The Development
of Western Music

An Anthology

Volume I

Second Edition

The Development of Western Music

An Anthology

Volume I
From Ancient Times through the Classical Era

Edited by

K   Marie   Stolba

Professor of Music, Emerita
Indiana University – Purdue
University at Fort Wayne

Madison, Wisconsin • Dubuque, Iowa

Book Team

Developmental Editor *Deborah D. Reinbold*
Production Editor *Suzanne M. Guinn*
Designer *Lu Ann Schrandt*
Permissions Coordinators *Vicki Krug and LouAnn Wilson*
Visuals/Design Developmental Consultant *Marilyn A. Phelps*
Visuals/Design Freelance Specialist *Mary L. Christianson*
Publishing Services Specialist *Sherry Padden*
Marketing Manager *Steven Yetter*
Advertising Manager *Nancy Milling*

Brown & Benchmark

A Division of Wm. C. Brown Communications, Inc.

Executive Vice President/General Manager *Thomas E. Doran*
Vice President/Editor in Chief *Edgar J. Laube*
Vice President/Sales and Marketing *Eric Ziegler*
Director of Production *Vickie Putman Caughron*
Director of Custom and Electronic Publishing *Chris Rogers*

Wm. C. Brown Communications, Inc.

President and Chief Executive Officer *G. Franklin Lewis*
Corporate Senior Vice President and Chief Financial Officer *Robert Chesterman*
Corporate Senior Vice President and President of Manufacturing *Roger Meyer*

Cover illustration by Jay Bryant

Consulting Editor Frederick W. Westphal

A Times Mirror Company

Library of Congress Catalog Card Number: 93–72779

ISBN 0–697–12549–1

Printed in the United States of America by Wm. C. Brown Communications, Inc., 2460 Kerper Boulevard, Dubuque, IA 52001

10 9 8 7 6 5 4 3 2 1

S. D. G.

Contents

Preface to the Second Edition

This second edition of *The Development of Western Music: An Anthology* is a two-volume historical anthology of music specifically designed to present music to be studied in conjunction with the second edition of the text *The Development of Western Music: A History*. With few exceptions, the selections are complete movements or complete compositions. The works are presented in the Anthology in the same order in which they are mentioned or discussed in the History text. Volume I contains selections representative of music from Ancient Times through the Classical Era; Volume II holds compositions characteristic of the transition from Classical to Romantic music, and Romantic and Modern works. Sets of sound recordings of the selections in the Anthology have been prepared and are available in either CD or cassette form for use with the Anthology and the History text. The music is printed in the Anthology in its original key; however, the recording, particularly of vocal music, may be in a different key. The recordings are intended to be a historical presentation; when feasible, recordings using period instruments have been selected. Because tuning was not standardized prior to 1700, there may be some instances in which the recorded music sounds "out of tune" to modern ears.

Texts of vocal music are presented in their original language, with English translation. Most of the translations of poetic and prose texts are my own; the work of other persons is acknowledged. I am indebted to Father Dick John of St. Francis College, Fort Wayne, for assistance with some medieval Latin texts containing particular ecclesiastical expressions, and to Miguel Roig-Francoli for help in translating some Spanish and Galician poetry.

Although this Anthology was designed to complement the History text, the Anthology is complete in itself, and its selections can serve as works for study and analysis in Form and Analysis, Music Literature, Music Theory, or other music courses.

It is impossible to name all those who contributed to this project. From time to time, several of my colleagues, particularly, John Loessi and Masson Robertson, have loaned me music from their personal libraries. Jody Smith graciously consented to copy into music calligraphy my transcriptions from manuscript. Many libraries have shared their holdings with me. Great demands have been made upon the Music Library at Indiana University, Bloomington, and thanks are due especially to Music Librarian R. Michael Fling, and the reference assistants, who responded promptly to my requests for materials. The librarians the Inter-Library Loan/Document Delivery Services department at Helmke Library, IPFW, were most helpful in procuring materials. Marilyn Grush spent much time helping me research sources at the OCLC station there. I wish to express my gratitude to Kenneth Balthaser, who made available the facilities the IPFW Learning Resource Center and the services of its technicians in the preparation of camera-ready proof, particularly, Roberta Sandy Shadle.

Where no specific modern publication is cited, the music was transcribed and/or edited from original sources. Brown & Benchmark and I are grateful the persons and publishers who have granted permission to reprint, edit, or adapt material for which they hold copyright. I wish to express my appreciation also to my editors at Brown & Benchmark, who carefully considered my requests and to my book team and all other persons who were involved in the production of these volumes.

K Marie Stolba
Fort Wayne, Indiana

1. A HURRIAN CULT SONG FROM ANCIENT UGARIT
Anonymous (c. 1400 B.C.)

Transcription and Arrangement
by Anne Draffkorn Kilmer

denotes broken or effaced portion of tablet

Because knowledge of the Hurrian language is still imperfect, no translation of these hymn lyrics is available. The word *nikala* indicates that the song is a hymn to the wife of the moon god, her name being Nikal (Nikkal). The words *wešal tatib tišya* translate "Thou lovest them in [thy] heart" and the closing words *Wewe ḫanuku* have been translated as "born of thee."

From Sounds from Silence, Berkley, CA

2. FIRST DELPHIC HYMN TO APOLLO
Anonymous (c. 130 B.C.)

Reproduced by permission of Oxford University Press.

Hearken, fair-armed daughters of Zeus the loud Thunderer, who have your appointed home on deep-wooded Helicon; come that you may honor with dance and song your brother, Phoebus of the golden tresses, who comes up to his abode on the twin peaks of this rock of Parnassus here, in the company of the far-famed women of Delphi, to visit the streams of Castalia with its fair waters, frequenting his prophetic hill upon the Delphic crag.

Behold! Attica's great and famous city, which by the prayers of the warrior maiden Tritonis dwells in a plain inviolate! On the holy altars the Firegod burns the thighs of young bulls, while the fragrance of Arabia is wafted to Olympus; and the flute in clear, shrill notes pipes its song with varied tunes; and the sweet-voiced lyre of gold strikes up the hymns.

But the whole swarm of musicians who have their home in Attica sing hymns of praise to you, famous player of the lyre, son of mighty Zeus, beside this your snow-capped hill; for you reveal to all mortals holy oracles which cannot lie, since you took the prophetic tripod which the fierce serpent used to guard, at that time when you pierced with your shafts its dappled, writhing form, until the monster, emitting harsh hisses thick and fast, breathed out its life likewise.

But when the War-god of the Celts. . . .

—Edna M. Hooker

3. EPITAPH OF SEIKILOS
(c. second century B.C.)

a. Greek Notation

C Z̄ Z̄ KIZ Ī
O-σον ζηις φαι νου

K̄ I Z IK O C̄ OΦ̄
μη-δὲν ὅ-λως σύ λυ-ποῦ

C K Z I KI K C̄ OΦ̄
πρὸς ὀ-λί-γον ἐσ-τὶ τὸ ζῆν

C K O I Z K C C̄ CXĪ
τὸ τέ-λος ὁ χρό-νος ἀπ-αι-τεῖ

b. Modern Transcription

As long as you live, be happy;
do not grieve at all.
Life's span is short;
time exacts the final reckoning.

3

4. SALVE, REGINA, Marian Antiphon
Anonymous

Gregorian Chant Notation

Modern Transcription

Salve, Regina, mater misericordiae:
Vita, dulcedo, et spes nostra, salve.
Ad te clamamus, exsules, filii Hevae.

Ad te suspiramus, gementes et flentes in
 hac lacrimarum valle.
Eia ergo, Advocata nostra, illos tuos
 misericordes oculos ad nos converte.
Et Jesum, benedictum fructum ventris tui,
 nobis post hoc exsilium ostende.
O clemens: O pia: O dulcis Virgo Maria.

Hail, Queen, compassionate mother:
Our life, sweetness, and hope, hail!
To you we cry aloud, exiles, children of
 Eve.
To you we send [our] sighs, groaning
 and weeping in this vale of tears.
Then, our Advocate, turn your
 compassionate eyes toward us.
And, after this exile, show us Jesus,
 the blessed fruit of your womb.
O merciful: O holy: O sweet Virgin
 Mary.

5. MISSA IN DOMINICA RESURRECTIONIS
(Mass for Easter Sunday)
Anonymous

Introit

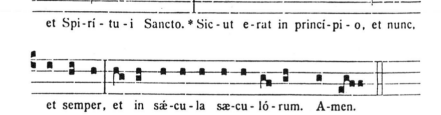

From LU, 788ff. Reprinted by permission of ABBAYE SAINT-PIERRE de SOLESMES, FRANCE.

Kyrie

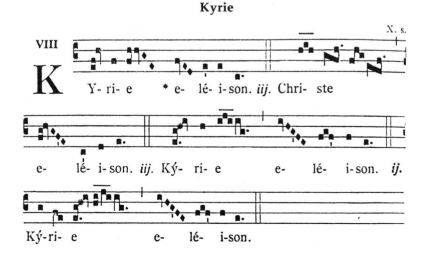

Gloria

IV X. s.

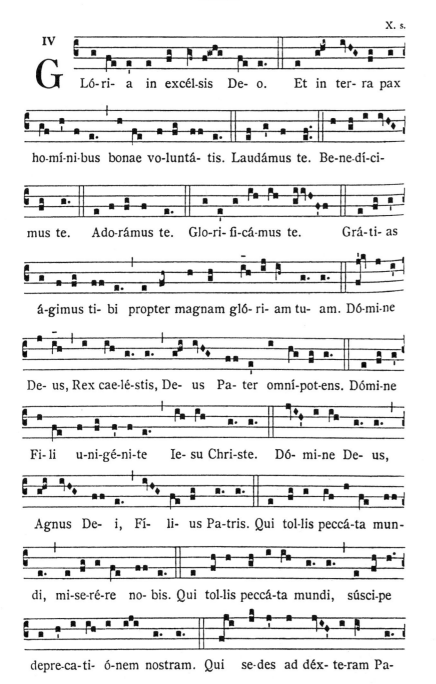

Gló-ri- a in excél-sis De- o. Et in ter- ra pax

ho-mí-ni-bus bonae vo-luntá- tis. Laudámus te. Be-ne-dí-ci-

mus te. Ado-rámus te. Glo-ri- fi-cá-mus te. Grá-ti- as

á-gimus ti- bi propter magnam gló- ri- am tu- am. Dó-mi-ne

De- us, Rex cae-lé-stis, De- us Pa- ter omní-pot-ens. Dómi-ne

Fi- li u-ni-gé-ni-te Ie- su Chri-ste. Dó- mi-ne De- us,

Agnus De- i, Fí- li- us Pa-tris. Qui tol-lis peccá-ta mun-

di, mi-se-ré-re no- bis. Qui tol-lis peccá-ta mundi, súsci-pe

depre-ca-ti- ó-nem nostram. Qui se-des ad déx-te-ram Pa-

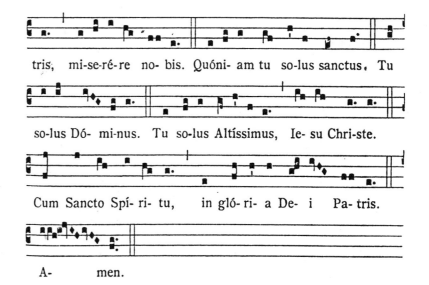

tris, mi-se-ré-re no- bis. Quóni- am tu so-lus sanctus. Tu

so-lus Dó- mi-nus. Tu so-lus Altíssimus, Ie- su Chri-ste.

Cum Sancto Spí- ri- tu, in gló- ri- a De- i Pa- tris.

A- men.

Collect

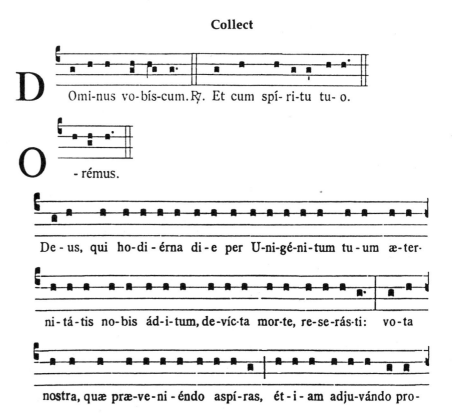

D Omi-nus vo-bís-cum. ℟. Et cum spí- ri-tu tu- o.

O - rémus.

De- us, qui ho-di- érna di- e per U-ni-gé-ni-tum tu- um æ-ter-

ni-tá-tis no-bis ád-i-tum, de-víc-ta mor-te, re-se-rás-ti: vo-ta

nostra, quæ præ-ve-ni- éndo aspí-ras, ét-i- am adju-vándo pro-

sé-que-re. Per e-ún-dem Dó-mi-num nostrum Je-sum Chris-tum,

Fí-li-um tu-um: Qui te-cum vi-vit et regnat in u-ni-tá-te

Spí-ri-tus Sanc-ti De-us, per óm-ni-a sǽ-cu-la sæ-cu-ló-rum.

℞. A-men.

Epistle

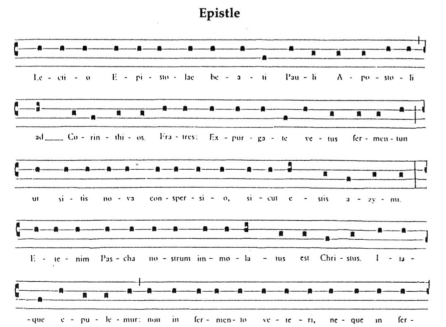

Lé-cti-o E-pí-sto-lae be-a-ti Pau-li A-po-sto-li

ad Co-rin-thi-os. Fra-tres: Ex-pur-ga-te ve-tus fer-men-tum

ut si-tis no-va con-sper-si-o, si-cut e-stis a-zy-mi.

E-te-nim Pas-cha no-strum im-mo-la-tus est Chri-stus. I-ta-

-que e-pu-le-mur: non in fer-men-to ve-te-ri, ne-que in fer-

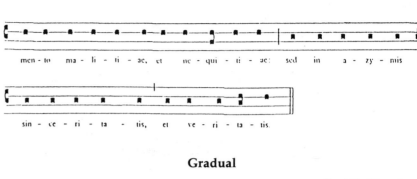

men-to ma-li-ti-ae, et ne-qui-ti-ae: sed in a-zy-mis

sin-ce-ri-ta-tis, et ve-ri-ta-tis.

Gradual

Ps. 117, 24 et 1

GR. II

Haec di-es, quam fe-cit

Dó-mi-nus: exsulté-mus,

et lae-té-mur in e-a.

℣. Confi-témi-ni Dó-mi-no,

quó-ni-am bo-nus:

quó-ni-am in saé-cu-lum

mi-se-ri-cór-di-a e-ius.

Alleluia

1 Cor. 5, 7

VII

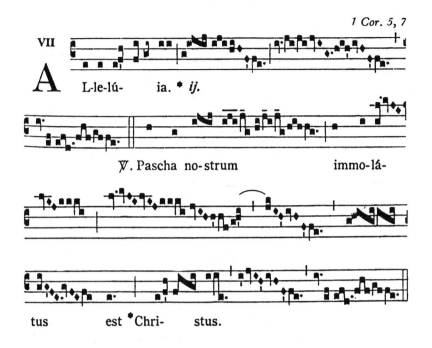

A L-le-lú- ia. * ij.

℣. Pascha no-strum immo-lá-

tus est *Chri- stus.

quid vi-dísti in vi- a? Sepúlcrum Christi vi-véntis, et gló-

ri- am vi-di re-surgéntis : Angé-li-cos testes, sudá-ri- um,

et vestes. Surré-xit Christus spes me- a : praecédet su-os in

Ga-li-laé- am. Scimus Christum surrexísse a mórtu- is ve-re :

tu no-bis, victor Rex, mi-se-ré-re. A -men. Al-le-lú-ja.

Sequence

SEQ. I

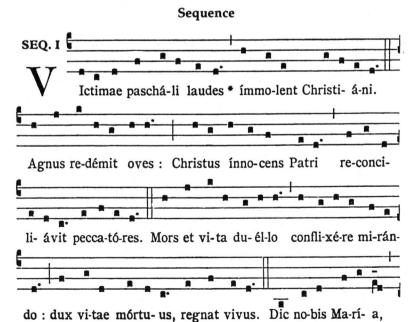

V Ictimae paschá-li laudes * ímmo-lent Christi- á-ni.

Agnus re-démit oves : Christus ínno-cens Patri re-conci-

li- ávit pecca-tó-res. Mors et vi-ta du-él-lo confli-xé-re mi-rán-

do : dux vi-tae mórtu- us, regnat vivus. Dic no-bis Ma-rí- a,

Gospel

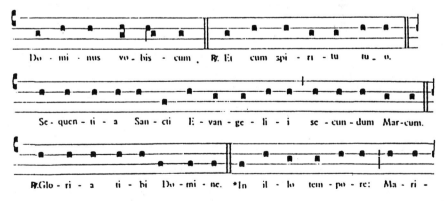

Do - mi - nus vo - bis - cum. ℟. Et cum spi - ri - tu tu - o.

Se - quen - ti - a San - cti E - van - ge - li - i se - cun - dum Mar-cum.

℟. Glo - ri - a ti - bi Do - mi - ne. *In il - lo tem - po - re: Ma - ri -

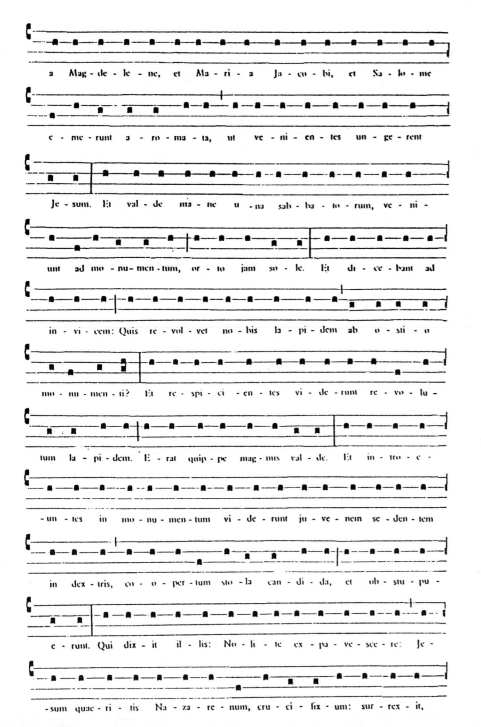

a Mag-de-le-ne, et Ma-ri-a Ja-co-bi, et Sa-lo-me

e-me-runt a-ro-ma-ta, ut ve-ni-en-tes un-ge-rent

Je-sum. Et val-de ma-ne u-na sab-ba-to-rum, ve-ni-

um ad mo-nu-men-tum, or-to jam so-le. Et di-ce-bant ad

in-vi-cem: Quis re-vol-vet no-bis la-pi-dem ab os-ti-o

mo-nu-men-ti? Et re-spi-ci-en-tes vi-de-runt re-vo-lu-

tum la-pi-dem. E-rat quip-pe mag-nus val-de. Et in-tro-e-

un-tes in mo-nu-men-tum vi-de-runt ju-ve-nem se-den-tem

in dex-tris, co-o-per-tum sto-la can-di-da, et ob-stu-pu-

e-runt. Qui dix-it il-lis: No-li-te ex-pa-ve-sce-re: Je-

-sum quae-ri-tis Na-za-re-num, cru-ci-fix-um: sur-rex-it,

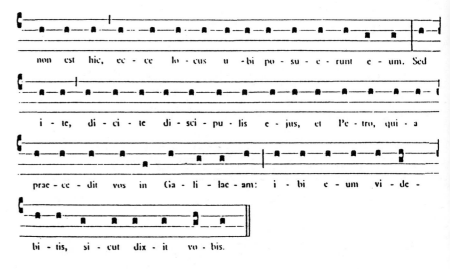

non est hic, ec-ce lo-cus u-bi po-su-e-runt e-um. Sed

i-te, di-ci-te di-sci-pu-lis e-jus, et Pe-tro, qui-a

prae-ce-dit vos in Ga-li-lae-am: i-bi e-um vi-de-

bi-tis, si-cut dix-it vo-bis.

Credo

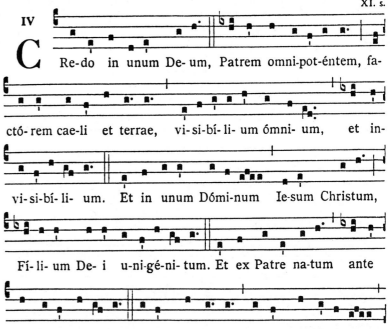

IV   XI. s.

C Re-do in unum De-um, Patrem omni-pot-éntem, fa-

ctó-rem cae-li et terrae, vi-si-bí-li-um ómni-um, et in-

vi-si-bí-li-um. Et in unum Dómi-num Ie-sum Christum,

Fí-li-um De-i u-ni-gé-ni-tum. Et ex Patre na-tum ante

ómni-a saécu-la. De-um de De-o, lumen de lúmine,

De- um ve-rum de De- o ve-ro. Gé-ni-tum, non factum, consub-

stanti- á-lem Patri : per quem ómni- a facta sunt. Qui pro-

pter nos hómi-nes, et propter nostram sa-lú-tem descéndit de

cae-lis. Et incarná-tus est de Spí-ri-tu Sancto ex Ma-rí- a

Vírgi- ne : Et homo factus est. Cru-ci- fí-xus ét-i- am pro

no-bis : sub Pónti- o Pi- lá-to passus, et sepúl-tus est. Et

re-surréxit térti- a di- e, se-cúndum Scriptú-ras. Et ascén-

dit in caelum : se-det ad déxte-ram Patris. Et í-te-rum ven-

tú-rus est cum gló-ri- a, iu-di-cá-re vivos et mórtu- os :

cu-ius regni non e- rit fi- nis. Et in Spí- ri- tum Sanctum,

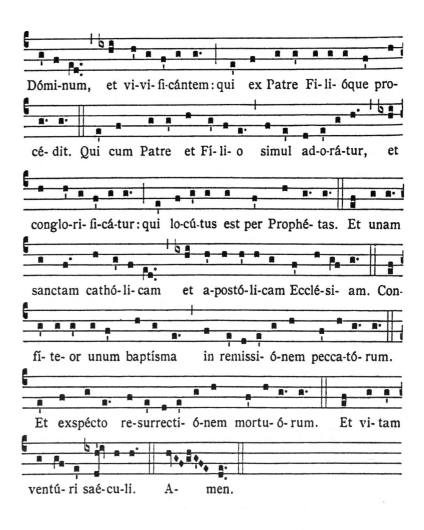

Dómi-num, et vi-vi-fi-cántem : qui ex Patre Fi- li- óque pro-

cé- dit. Qui cum Patre et Fí- li- o simul ad-o-rá-tur, et

conglo-ri- fi-cá-tur : qui lo-cú-tus est per Prophé- tas. Et unam

sanctam cathó-li- cam et a-postó-li-cam Ecclé-si- am. Con-

fí- te- or unum baptísma in remissi- ó-nem pecca-tó- rum.

Et exspécto re-surrecti- ó-nem mortu- ó- rum. Et vi- tam

ventú- ri saé-cu-li. A- men.

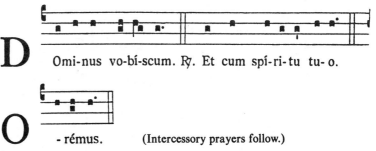

D Omi-nus vo-bí-scum. ℟. Et cum spí-ri-tu tu- o.

O - rémus. (Intercessory prayers follow.)

Offertory

OF. IV · Ps. 75, 9. 10

Terra *tré-mu-it, et qui-é-vit,

dum re-súrge-ret in iudí-ci-o De-us,

al- le- lú-ia.

Secret (spoken)

Suscipe, quaesumus Domine, preces populi tui
cum oblationibus hostiarum: ut paschalibus initiata
mysteriis, ad aeternitatis nobis medelam, te operante, proficiant. Per
Dominum . . .

℟ Amen.

Preface

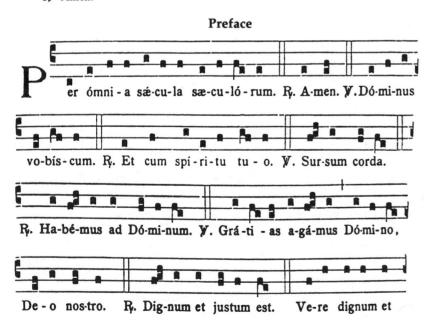

Per ómni-a sǽ-cu-la sæ-cu-ló-rum. ℟. A-men. ℣. Dó-mi-nus

vo-bís-cum. ℟. Et cum spi-ri-tu tu-o. ℣. Sur-sum corda.

℟. Ha-bé-mus ad Dó-mi-num. ℣. Grá-ti-as a-gá-mus Dó-mi-no,

De-o nos-tro. ℟. Dig-num et justum est. Ve-re dignum et

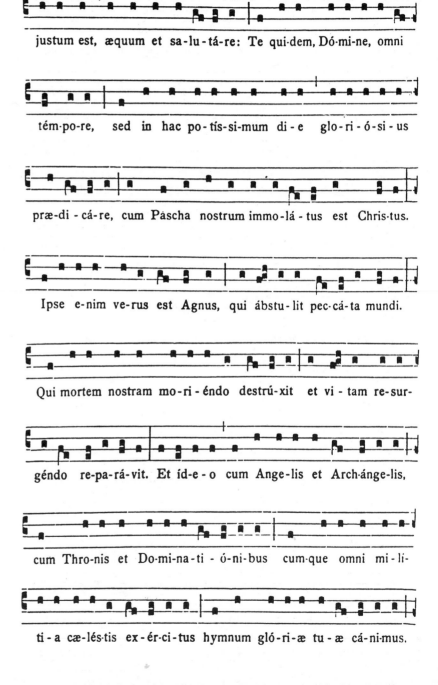

justum est, æquum et sa-lu-tá-re: Te qui-dem, Dó-mi-ne, omni

tém-po-re, sed in hac po-tís-si-mum di-e glo-ri-ó-si-us

præ-di-cá-re, cum Páscha nostrum immo-lá-tus est Chris-tus.

Ipse e-nim ve-rus est Agnus, qui ábstu-lit pec-cá-ta mundi.

Qui mortem nostram mo-ri-éndo destrú-xit et vi-tam re-sur-

géndo re-pa-rá-vit. Et íd-e-o cum Ange-lis et Arch-ánge-lis,

cum Thro-nis et Do-mi-na-ti-ó-ni-bus cum-que omni mi-li-

ti-a cæ-lés-tis ex-ér-ci-tus hymnum gló-ri-æ tu-æ cá-ni-mus.

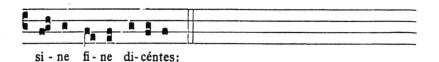

si - ne fi - ne di - céntes:

Sanctus

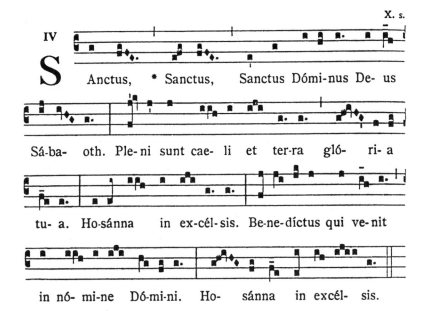

X. s.

IV

SAnctus, * Sanctus, Sanctus Dómi-nus De- us

Sá-ba- oth. Ple-ni sunt cae- li et ter-ra gló- ri- a

tu- a. Ho-sánna in ex-cél- sis. Be-ne-díctus qui ve-nit

in nó- mi-ne Dó-mi-ni. Ho- sánna in excél- sis.

Canon, Pater Noster

Per óm-ni- a sǽ-cu-la sæ-cu-ló- rum. ℟. Amen.

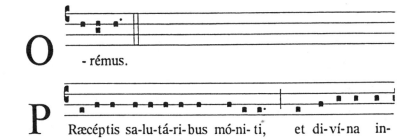

O- rémus.

PRæcéptis sa-lu-tá-ri-bus mó-ni- ti, et di-ví-na in-

sti-tu-ti- óne formá- ti, audémus dí-ce-re :

Pa-ter noster, qui es in cæ-lis : sancti- fi-cé- tur nomen

tu- um; advé-ni- at regnum tu- um; fi- at vo-lúntas tu- a,

sic-ut in cæ-lo, et in terra. Panem nostrum co-ti-di- á-

num da no-bis hó-di- e; et dimítte no-bis dé-bi-ta nostra,

sic-ut et nos dimít-timus de-bi-tó-ri-bus nostris; et ne nos

indú-cas in tenta-ti- ó- nem; sed lí-be-ra nos a ma- lo.

Per ómni- a sǽ-cu-la sæ-cu-ló- rum. ℟. Amen.

PAX Dómi- ni sit semper vo-bís-cum. ℟. Et cum spí-

ri-tu tu- o.

Agnus Dei

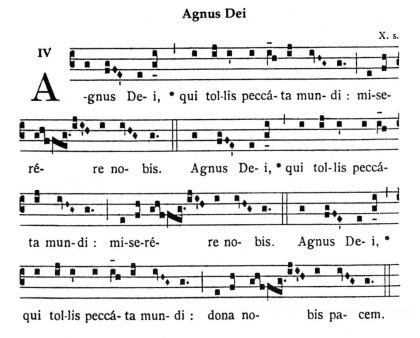

X. s.

Agnus De- i, * qui tol·lis peccá- ta mun- di : mi-se-

ré- re no- bis. Agnus De- i, * qui tol·lis peccá-

ta mun- di : mi-se-ré- re no- bis. Agnus De- i, *

qui tol·lis peccá- ta mun- di : dona no- bis pa- cem.

Communion

1 Cor. 5, 7. 8

CO. VI

Pascha nostrum * immo-lá-tus est Chri-

stus, alle-lú- ia : í-ta- que e-pu-lé- mur

in á- zy-mis since-ri-tá-tis et ve-ri-tá- tis, alle-

lú- ia, alle- lú- ia, al-le- lú- ia.

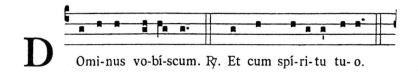

DOmi-nus vo-bí-scum. ℟. Et cum spí-ri-tu tu- o.

Postcommunion

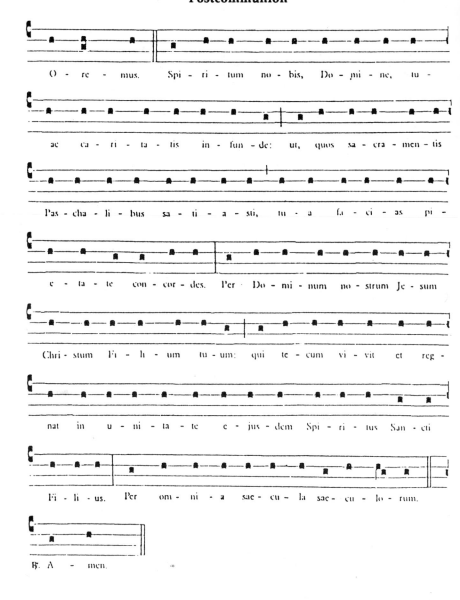

O- re- mus. Spi-ri-tum no-bis, Do-mi-ne, tu-

ac ca-ri-ta-tis in-fun-de: ut, quos sa-cra-men-tis

Pas-cha-li-bus sa-ti-a-sti, tu-a fa-ci-as pi-

e-ta-te con-cor-des. Per Do-mi-num no-strum Je-sum

Chri-stum Fi-li-um tu-um: qui te-cum vi-vit et reg-

nat in u-ni-ta-te e-jus-dem Spi-ri-tus San-cti

Fi-li-us. Per om-ni-a sae-cu-la sae-cu-lo-rum.

℟. A- men.

Dismissal

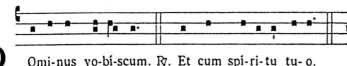

D Omi-nus vo-bí-scum. ℟. Et cum spí-ri-tu tu- o.

VIII

I -te, missa est, alle-lú-ia, alle- lú- ia.
De-o grá-ti- as, alle-lú-ia, alle- lú- ia.

INTROIT

Resurrexi, et adhuc tecum sum, alleluia:

posuisti super me manum tuam, alleluia:

mirabilis facta est scientia tua, alleluia, alleluia.

Ps.
Domine probasti me, et cognovisti me:

tu cognovisti sessionem meam, et resurrectionem meam.

Gloria Patri et Filio, et Spiritu Sancto.

Sicut erat in principio, et nunc, et semper, et in saecula saeculorum.* Amen.

I have risen, and I am still with thee, alleluia:

thou hast laid thy hand upon me, alleluia:

thy knowledge has done wonderful things, alleluia, alleluia.

Psalm [138/139: 1–2]
Lord, thou has proven me, and thou hast known me:

thou hast known my sitting down, and my rising up.

Glory be to the Father and to the Son, and to the Holy Spirit.

As it was in the beginning, and [is] now, and always [= and ever shall be], and through ages of ages.* Amen.

*sometimes translated as "world without end"

KYRIE

Kyrie eleison.
Christe eleison.
Kyrie eleison.

Lord have mercy.
Christ have mercy.
Lord have mercy.

GLORIA

Gloria in excelsis Deo.
Et in terra pax hominibus bonae voluntatis.

Laudamus te.
Benedicimus te.
Adoramus te.
Glorificamus te.
Gratias agimus tibi propter magnam gloriam tuam.

Domine Deus, Rex caelestis, Deus Pater omnipotens.

Domine Fili unigenite Jesu Christe.
Domine Deus, Agnus Dei, Filius Patris.

Qui tollis peccata mundi, miserere nobis.

Qui tollis peccata mundi, suscipe deprecationem nostram.
Qui sedes ad dexteram Patris, miserere nobis.
Quoniam tu solus sanctus.
Tu solus Dominus.
Tu solus Altissimus, Jesu Christe.
Cum Sancto Spiritu, in gloria Dei Patris.
Amen.

Glory to God in the highest.
And on earth peace to men of good will.

We praise thee.
We bless thee.
We adore thee.
We glorify thee.
We give thee thanks for thy great glory.

Lord God, King of heaven, God the Father almighty.

Lord, the only-begotten Son, Jesus Christ.
Lord God, Lamb of God, Son of the Father.

[Thou] Who takest away the sins of the world, have mercy on us.

[Thou] Who takest away the sins of the world, receive our prayer.

[Thou] Who sittest at the right hand of the Father, have mercy on us.

Because thou alone [art] holy.
Thou alone [art] Lord.
Thou alone [art] Most High, Jesus Christ.
With the Holy Spirit, in the glory of God the Father.
Amen.

COLLECT

Dominus vobiscum.
℟ Et cum spiritu tuo.

Oremus.

Deus, qui hodierna die per Unigenitum tuum, aeternitatis nobis aditum devicta morte reserasti:

vota nostra, quae praeveniendo aspiras, etiam adjuvando prosequere.
Per eundem Dominum nostrum Jesum Christum, Filium tuum:
qui tecum vivit et regnat in unitate Spiritus Sancti Deus, per omnia saecula saeculorum.
℟ Amen.

The Lord be with you.
℟ And with thy spirit.

Let us pray.

God, who this day through thy only-begotten Son, conquered death, you have opened to us the gate of eternity [= everlasting life]:

help us attain [or, fulfill] our desires, which thou dost inspire.
Through the same Jesus Christ, our Lord, thy Son:
who with thee lives and reigns God in the unity of the Holy Spirit, through all ages of ages [= for ever].
℟ Amen.

EPISTLE (I Cor. 5:7–8)

Lectio Epistolae beati Pauli Apostoli ad Corinthios.

A reading from the Epistle of the blessed apostle Paul to the Corinthians.

Fratres: Expurgate vetus fermentum, ut sitis nova conspersio, sicut estis azymi. Etenim Pascha nostrum immolatus est Christus.

Brethren: Purge out the old leaven, so that you may be a new mixture [literally, temperament], as you are unleavened. For Christ, our Passover, has been sacrificed.

Itaque epulemur: non in fermento veteri, neque in fermento malitiae, et nequitiae: sed in azymis sinceritatis, et veritatis.

Therefore, let us feast: not with the old leaven, nor with the leaven of malice, and wickedness, but with the unleavened [bread] of sincerity, and truth.

GRADUAL

Haec dies, quam fecit Dominus: exsultemus, et laetemur in ea.

This is the day which the Lord hath made: we will rejoice, and let us be glad in it.

℣ Confitemini Domino, quoniam bonus; quoniam in saeculum misericordia ejus.

℣ Confess* to the Lord, for He is good; for His mercy [endures] for ever.

*Literally, confess; however, in The Bible the verse is variously translated as "Praise the Lord" and "Give thanks to the Lord." (Psalm 135/136:1)

ALLELUIA

Alleluia. (3 times)

Alleluia.

℣ Pascha nostrum immolatus est Christus.

℣ Christ, our Passover, has been sacrificed.

SEQUENCE

Victimae paschali laudes immolent Christiani.

To the Paschal Victim let Christians offer songs of praise.

Agnus redemit oves: Christus innocens Patri reconciliavit peccatores.

The Lamb has redeemed the sheep: sinless Christ has reconciled sinners to the Father.

Mors et vita duello conflixere mirando: dux vitae mortuus, regnat vivus.

Death and life have clashed in a miraculous combat: the leader of life died, [yet] living he reigns.

Dic nobis Maria, quid vidisti in via? Sepulchrum Christi viventis, et gloriam vidi resurgentis: Angelicos testes, sudarium, et vestes.

Tell us, Mary, what you saw on the way? I saw the tomb of the living Christ, and the glory of [His] resurrection: The angel witnesses, the napkin, and the grave-clothes.

Surrexit Christus spes mea: praecedet suos in Galilaeam. Scimus Christum surrexisse a mortuis vere: tu nobis, victor Rex, miserere.

Christ, my hope, has risen: he precedes his own into Galilee. We know Christ has truly risen from the dead: Thou, victor King, have mercy on us.

Amen. Alleluia.

Amen. Alleluia.

GOSPEL (Mark 16:1–7)

Dominus vobiscum.
℟ Et cum spiritu tuo.

The Lord be with you.
℟ And with thy spirit.

Sequentia sancti Evangelii secundum Marcum.
℟ Gloria tibi Domine.

Next, [reading] from the holy Gospel according to Mark.
℟ Glory to Thee, Lord.

In illo tempore:
Maria Magdalene, et Maria Jacobi, et Salome emerunt aromata, ut venientes ungerent Jesum.

At that time:
Mary Magdalene, and Mary [the mother] of James, and Salome bought spices, in order that they might come and anoint Jesus.

Et valde mane una sabbatorum, veniunt ad monumentum, orto jam sole.

And very early in the morning on the first day of the week, they came to the tomb, at sunrise.

Et dicebant ad invicem: Quis revolvet nobis lapidem ab ostio monumenti?

And they said to one another: Who will roll away for us the stone from the door of the sepulchre?

Et respicientes viderunt revolutum lapidem.
Erat quippe magnus valde.

And, looking, they saw the stone [had been] rolled back.
Certainly, it was very large.

Et introeuntes in monumentum viderunt juvenem sedentem in dextris, coopertum stola candida, et obstupuerunt.

And entering the sepulchre, they saw a young man sitting on the right side, clothed in a long, dazzling white robe, and they were astonished.

Qui dicit illis: Nolite expavescere: Jesum quaeritis Nazarenum, crucifixum: surrexit, non est hic, ecce locus ubi posuerunt eum.

He said to them: Do not be exceedingly frightened: You seek Jesus of Nazareth, [who was] crucified: He has risen; he is not here; behold the place where they laid him.

Sed ite, dicite discipulis ejus, et Petro, quia praecedit vos in Galilaeam: ibi eum videbitis, sicut dixit vobis.

But go, tell his disciples, and Peter, he precedes you into Galilee: there you will see him, as he told you.

CREDO

Credo in unum Deum.

Patrem omnipotentem, factorem caeli et terrae, visibilium omnium et invisibilium.

Et in unum Dominum Jesum Christum, Filium Dei unigenitum.

Et ex Patre natum, ante omnia saecula.

Deum de Deo, lumen de lumine, Deum verum de Deo vero.

Genitum, non factum, consubstantialem Patri: per quem omnia facta sunt.

Qui propter nos homines et propter nostram salutem descendit de caelis.

Et incarnatus est de Spiritu Sancto ex Maria Virgine: Et homo factus est.

Crucifixus etiam pro nobis: sub Pontio Pilato passus et sepultus est.

Et resurrexit tertia die, secundum Scripturas.

Et ascendit in caelum: sedet ad dexteram Patris.

Et iterum venturus est cum gloria judicare vivos et mortuos: cujus regni non erit finis.

Et in Spiritum Sanctum, Dominum, et vivificantem: qui ex Patre Filioque procedit.

Qui cum Patre et Filio simul adoratur et conglorificatur: qui locutus est per Prophetas.

Et unam sanctam catholicam et apostolicam Ecclesiam.

Confiteor unum baptisma in remissionem peccatorum.

Et exspecto resurrectionem mortuorum. Et vitam venturi saeculi.

Amen.

Dominus vobiscum.

R⁷ Et cum spiritu tuo.

Oremus.

I believe in one God.

The Father almighty, maker of heaven and earth, [and] of all things visible and invisible.

And in one Lord, Jesus Christ, only-begotten Son of God.

And born of the Father, before all ages.

God from God, light from light, true God from true God.

Born, not made, of one substance with the Father: through whom all things were made.

Who for us men [i.e., mankind] and for our salvation came down from heaven.

And was made incarnate by the Holy Spirit of the Virgin Mary: And was made man.

Also, he was crucified for us: he suffered under Pontius Pilate and was buried.

And he rose again on the third day, according to the Scriptures.

And he ascended into heaven: he sits at the right hand of the Father.

And he will come again with glory to judge the living and the dead: of his kingdom there will be no end.

And in the Holy Spirit, Lord, and giver of life: who proceeds from the Father and the Son.

Who, together with the Father and the Son, is worshiped and glorified: who spoke through the prophets.

And in one holy, universal, and apostolic church.

I confess* one baptism in remission of sins. [*or, I acknowledge one baptism. . . .]

And I look forward to the resurrection of the dead. And life in the ages to come.

Amen.

The Lord be with you.

R⁷ And with thy spirit.

Let us pray. [Prayers follow.]

OFFERTORY (Ps. 75/76:9,10)

Terra tremuit, et quievit,
dum resurgeret in judicio Deus,
alleluia.

The earth trembled, and was still,
when God rose in judgment,
alleluia.

SECRET

Suscipe, quaesumus Domine, preces populi tui cum oblationis hostiarum:

ut paschalibus initiata mysteriis, ad aeternitatis nobis medelem, te operante, proficiant. Per Dominum . . .

R⁷ Amen.

Accept, we beseech thee, Lord, the prayers of thy people together with the sacrifice they offer:

that what has been begun by these Easter mysteries may by thy working profit us to everlasting salvation. Through our Lord . . .

R⁷ Amen.

PREFACE

Per omnia saecula saeculorum.

R⁷ Amen.

Dominus vobiscum.

R. Et cum spiritu tuo.

Sursum corda.

R⁷ Habemus ad Dominum.

Gratias agamus Domino, Deo nostro.

R⁷ Dignum et justum est.

Vere dignum et justum est, aequum et salutare:

Te quidem, Domine, omni tempore, sed in hac potissimum die gloriosius praedicare: cum Pascha nostrum immolatus est Christus.

Ipse enim verus est Agnus, qui abstulit peccata mundi.

Qui mortem nostram moriendo destruxit et vitam resurgendo reparavit.

Et ideo cum Angelis et Archangelis, cum Thronis et Dominationibus cumque omni militia caelestis exercitus hymnum gloriae tuae canimus, sine fine dicentes:

For ever and ever. (or, Through all ages of ages.)

R⁷ Amen.

The Lord be with you.

R. And with thy spirit.

Lift up your hearts.

R⁷ We have [lifted them up] to the Lord.

Let us give thanks to the Lord, our God.

R⁷ It is fitting and just.

It is truly fitting and just, right and profitable:

Indeed, to praise thee, Lord, at all times, but chiefly on this glorious day when Christ, our Passover, has been sacrificed for us.

For he is the true Lamb, who has taken away the sins of the world.

Who, dying, destroyed our death, and, rising again, he has restored [our] life.

And, therefore, with the angels and archangels, with thrones and dominations, and with all the array of the heavenly hosts, we sing a hymn to thy glory, unceasingly chanting:

SANCTUS

Sanctus, Sanctus, Sanctus Dominus Deus Sabaoth.
Pleni sunt caeli et terra gloria tua.
Hosanna in excelsis.
Benedictus qui venit in nomine Domini.

Hosanna in excelsis.

Holy, Holy, Holy, Lord God of Sabaoth.
Heaven and earth are full of thy glory.
Hosanna in the highest.
Blessed [is he] who comes in the name of the Lord.
Hosanna in the highest.

CANON, PATER NOSTER

Per omnia saecula saeculorum.

R/ Amen.

For ever and ever. [or, Through ages of ages.]
R/ Amen.

Oremus:
Praeceptis salutaribus moniti, et divina institutione formati, audemus dicere:

Pater noster, qui es in caelis:
Sanctificetur nomen tuum:
Adveniat regnum tuum:
Fiat voluntas tua, sicut in caelo, et in terra.
Panem nostrum cotidianum da nobis hodie:
Et dimitte nobis debita nostra, sicut et nos dimittimus debitoribus nostris.

Et ne nos inducas in tentationem.
Sed libera nos a malo.

Let us pray:
Admonished by wholesome precepts, and patterned by divine instruction, we dare to say:
Our Father, who art in heaven:
Hallowed be thy name:
Thy kingdom come:
Thy will be done, as in heaven, so on earth.

Give us today our daily bread:

And forgive us our debts [trespasses], as we forgive our debtors [those who trespass against us].
And lead us not into temptation.
But deliver us from evil.

Per omnia saecula saeculorum.
R/ Amen.
Pax Domini sit semper vobiscum.
R/ Et cum spiritu tuo.

For ever and ever. [Through ages of ages.]
R/ Amen.
The peace of the Lord be with you always.
R/ And with thy spirit.

COMMUNION

Pascha nostrum immolatus est Christus, alleluia:
itaque epulemur in azymis sinceritatis et veritatis,
alleluia, alleluia, alleluia.

Christ, our Passover, has been sacrificed, alleluia:
therefore, let us feast with the unleavened [bread] of sincerity and truth,
alleluia, alleluia, alleluia.

Dominus vobiscum.
R/ Et cum spiritu tuo.

The Lord be with you.
R/ And with thy spirit.

POSTCOMMUNION

Oremus.

Spiritum nobis Domine, tuae caritatis infunde: ut, quos sacramentis paschalibus satiasti, tua facias pietate concordes.

Per Dominum nostrum Jesum Christum Filium tuum, qui tecum vivit et regnat in unitate ejusdem Spiritus Sancti Filius.
Per omnia saecula saeculorum.
R/ Amen.

Dominus vobiscum.
R/ Et cum spiritu tuo.

Let us pray.

God, impart to us the spirit of your love: so that, [those] whom thou hast fed with the Paschal sacrament, may be brought into harmony by thy compassion.
Through our Lord, Jesus Christ, thy Son, who lives and reigns with you in the same unity of the Holy Spirit.

For ever and ever. [Through ages of ages.]
R/ Amen.

The Lord be with you.
R/ And with thy spirit.

DISMISSAL

Ite, missa est, alleluia, alleluia.

R/ Deo gratias, alleluia, alleluia.

Go, it [the message] has been sent, alleluia, alleluia.
R/ Thanks be to God, alleluia, alleluia.

6. ABSOLVE, DOMINE, Tract
Anonymous

Absolve, Domine, animas omnium
fidelium defunctorum ab omni
vinculo delictorum.

℣ Et gratia tua illis succurrente,
mereantur evadere judicium ultionis.

℣ Et lucis aeternae beatitudine perfrui.

Lord, absolve [or, deliver] the souls of
all of the faithful departed
[deceased] from every bond of [their]
sins.

℣ And, assisted in that by your grace,
may they merit escaping [or, be able
to escape] the judgment of
punishment.

℣ And enjoy to the full the blessing of
eternal light.

From LU, 1809. Reprinted by permission of ABBAYE SAINT-PIERRE de SOLESMES, FRANCE.

7. DIES IRAE, Sequence
Thomas of Celano (c. 1200-1250)

From LU, 1810-1813. Reprinted by permission of ABBAYE SAINT-PIERRE de SOLESMES, FRANCE.

Quid sum mí-ser tunc dictúrus? Quem patró-num roga-tú-

rus? Cum vix jústus sit secúrus. Rex treméndae ma-je-

stá-tis, Qui sal-vándos sálvas gra-tis, Sálva me, fons pi-e-

tá-tis. Recordá-re Jé-su pí-e, Quod sum cáusa tú-ae

ví-ae : Ne me pér-das illa dí-e. Quaérens me, se-dí-

sti lássus : Redemísti crúcem pássus : Tántus lá-bor non

sit cássus. Júste júdex ul-ti-ónis, Dó-num fac remissi-ó-

nis, Ante dí-em ra-ti-ónis. Ingemísco, tamquam

ré-us : Cúlpa rúbet vúltus mé-us : Suppli-cánti párce

Dé-us. Qui Ma-rí-am absolvísti, Et latró-nem exau-

dísti, Mí-hi quoque spem dedísti. Préces mé-ae non sunt

dígnae : Sed tu bó-nus fac benígne, Ne per-énni crémer

ígne. Inter óves ló-cum praésta, Et ab haédis me

sequéstra, Stá-tu-ens in párte déxtra. Confu-tá-tis ma-

ledíctis, Flámmis ácribus addíctis, Vóca me cum be-

nedíctis. Oro súpplex et acclí-nis, Cor contrí-tum qua-

si cí-nis : Gé-re cúram mé-i fí-nis. Lacrimósa dí-es

illa, Qua resúrget ex favílla Judi-cándus hó-mo

ré-us : Hú-ic ergo pár-ce Dé-us. Pí-e Jésu Dómine,

dóna é-is réqui-em. A-men.

Dies irae, dies illa,
Solvet saeclum in favilla:

Teste David cum Sibylla.

Day of wrath, that day
the world comes to an end in glowing
    ashes:
attested [i.e., prophesied] by David and
    the Sibyl.

Quantus tremor est futurus,
Quando judex est venturus,
Cuncta stricte discussurus.

How great the trembling will be,
when the judge arrives,
[who] will put an end to all things by
    strict letter of the law.

Tuba mirum spargens sonum

Per sepulcra regionum,
Coget omnes ante thronum.

The war-trumpet pouring forth
    wondrous sound
through the tombs of the region,
will gather all (or, everything) before
    the throne.

Mors stupebit et natura,
Cum resurget creatura,
Judicanti responsura.

Death and Nature will be astonished,
when [all] creation rises again,
Responding for judgment.

Liber scriptus proferetur,
In quo totum continetur,
Unde mundus judicetur.

A written book will be brought forth,
in which everything will be contained,
from which the world will be judged.

Judex ergo cum sedebit,
Quidquid latet apparebit,

Nil inultum remanebit.

Then, when the judge is seated,
whatever is hidden will be made
    manifest;
nothing will remain unavenged.

Quid sum miser tunc dicturus?
Quem patronum rogaturus?
Cum vix justus sit securus.

What shall a wretch such as I say then?
Of what patron shall I ask help,
when the just (or, righteous) are
    scarcely secure?

Rex tremendae majestatis,

Qui salvandos salvas gratis,
Salva me, fons pietatis.

King of fearful (or, awe-inspiring)
    majesty,
who freely saves the redeemed,
save me, [O] fountain of mercy.
    [literally, respected source]

Recordare, Jesu pie,
Quod sum causa tuae viae:

Ne me perdas illa die.

Remember, holy Jesus,
that I am the cause of your course of
    action [i.e., your life on earth]:
Do not forsake me on that day.

Quaerens me, sedisti lassus:
Redemisti crucem passus:

Tantus labor non sit cassus.

Seeking me, you have sat down, weary:
Outstretched on the cross, you have
    ransomed [me]:
Let not such effort be in vain.

Juste judex ultionis,
Donum fac remissionis,
Ante diem rationis.

Just avenging judge,
make the gift of remission,
before the day of reckoning.

Ingemisco, tamquam reus:

Culpa rubet vultus meus:
Supplicanti parce, Deus.

I groan, as such a defendant (or, one
    accused):
My countenance reddens with guilt:
[O] God, spare the suppliant (or, the
    one earnestly entreating).

Qui Mariam absolvisti,
Et latronem exaudisti,
Mihi quoque spem dedisti.

[You] Who have absolved Mary,
and have listened to the thief,
have given me hope, also.

Preces meae non sunt dignae,
Sed tu bonus fac benigne,

Ne perenni cremer igne.

My prayers are not worthy,
but You [who are] good, act
    benevolently
not to consume [my soul] in eternal fire.

Inter oves locum praesta,
Et ab haedis me sequestra,
Statuens in parte dextra.

Offer me a place among the sheep,
and sequester me from the goats,
causing me to stand in the portion at
    your right hand.

Confutatis maledictis,
Flammis acribus addictis,
Voca me cum benedictis.

The evil ones having been repressed,
doomed to bitter flames,
call me with the blessed.

Oro supplex et acclinis,
Cor contritum quasi cinis:
Gere curam mei finis.

I pray, suppliant, and kneeling,
heart contrite, as if in ashes:
bear in Your care my ending.

Lacrimosa dies illa,
Qua resurget ex favilla

Judicandus homo reus:
Huic ergo parce Deus.

That sorrowful day,
when, from the ashes, mankind will rise
    again
bound for judgment:
Then, God, spare him.

Pie Jesu Domine,
dona eis requiem.

Merciful Lord Jesus,
give them rest.

Amen.

Amen.

8. QUEM QUAERITIS IN SEPULCHRO?
Anonymous

ANGEL
Quem quaeritis in sepulchro, O
Christicolae?

THREE WOMEN
Jesum Nazarenum crucifixum, O
coelicola.

Reproduced by permission of Oxford University Press.

ANGEL
Whom do you seek in the sepulchre, O
followers of Christ?

THREE WOMEN
Jesus of Nazareth, [who was] crucified, O
celestial one.

ANGEL
Non est hic, surrexit sicut predixerat;
ite, nuntiate quia surrexit, dicentes:

WOMEN
Alleluia, resurrexit Dominus hodie, leo
fortis, Christus filius Dei, Deo
gratias, dicite eia!

ANGEL
Venite et videte locum ubi positus erat
Dominus, Alleluia, alleluia. Cito
euntes, dicite discipulis quia surrexit
Dominus. Alleluia, alleluia.

WOMEN
Surrexit Dominus de sepulchro, qui pro
nobis pependit in ligno. Alleluia.

ANGEL
He is not here, he is risen as he predicted;
go, announce that he is risen, saying:

WOMEN
Alleluia, the Lord is risen today, the strong
lion, Christ the son of God, thanks be to
God, say "Eia!"

ANGEL
Come and see the place where the Lord
was laid! Alleluia, alleluia. Go quickly,
tell the disciples that the Lord is risen.
Alleluia, alleluia.

WOMEN
The Lord is risen from the sepulchre, who
for us hung on the cross. Alleluia.

9. UT QUEANT LAXIS
Guido d'Arezzo (c. 990–1050)

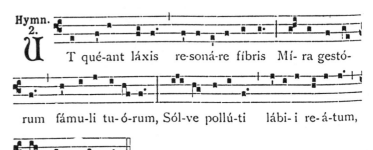

Ut queant laxis resonare fibris
   Mira gestorum famuli tuorum,
Solve polluti labii reatum,
   Sancte Johannes.

—attributed to Paul Diacré
   (c. 730–c. 799)

So that the wonders of your deeds [while] in
   servitude are able to resound,
Be acquitted of the accusation of depraved
   lips, Saint John.

From LU, 1504, Reprinted by permission of Abbaye Saint-Pierre de Solesmes, France.

10. EARLY ORGANUM, Examples from ninth-century treatise
Musica enchiriadis, Anonymous

a. TU PATRIS SEMPITERNUS ES FILIUS, Strict simple organum

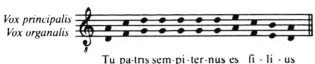

Tu pa-tris sem-pi-ter-nus es fi-li-us
You are the everlasting son of the Father.

b. TU PATRIS SEMPITERNUS ES FILIUS, Strict composite organum

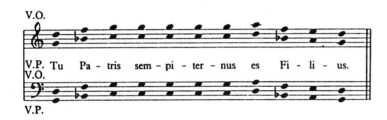

Tu Patris sempiternus es Filius.
—from the *Te Deum laudamus.*

You are the everlasting Son of the Father.

c. REX CAELI, Modified parallel organum

Rex caeli, Domine maris undisoni
Titanis nitidi squalidique soli,
Te humiles famuli modulis venerando
   piis
Se jubeas flagitant variis liberare malis.

King of heaven, Lord of the roaring sea,
of the dark earth and the shining sun,
Your humble servants by worshiping with
   pious phrases,
Entreat You to free them, by Your
   command, from [their] various ills.

11. FREE ORGANUM

ALLELUIA, JUSTUS UT PALMA, from Anonymous treatise
Ad organum faciendum (c. 1100)

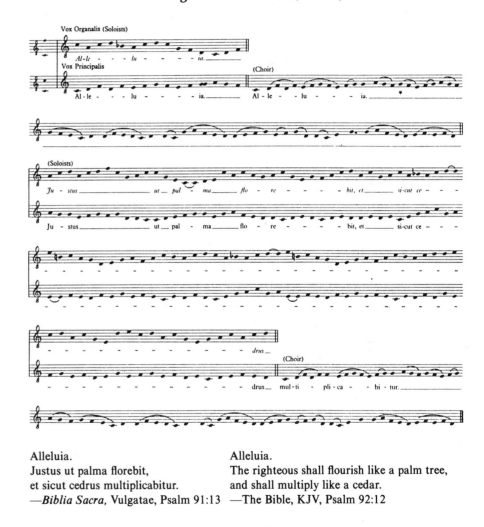

Alleluia.
Justus ut palma florebit,
et sicut cedrus multiplicabitur.
—*Biblia Sacra,* Vulgatae, Psalm 91:13

Alleluia.
The righteous shall flourish like a palm tree,
and shall multiply like a cedar.
—The Bible, KJV, Psalm 92:12

12. BENEDICAMUS [DOMINO], St. Martial style organum
Anonymous

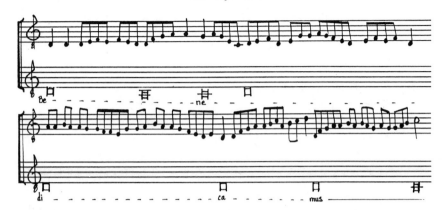

Benedicamus [Domino]   Let us bless [the Lord]

From MS Lat. 1139, fol. 41, Reprinted by permission of Abbaye Saint-Pierre de Solesmes, France.

13. ALLELUIA, PASCHA NOSTRUM

a. Chant

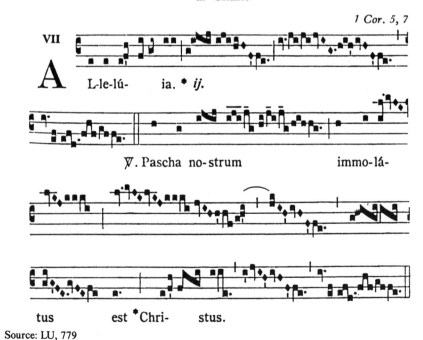

Source: LU, 779

b. Chant with Discant-style Organum Duplum and Clausulae
by Léonin (fl. c. 1163-1190)

Soloists:

Choir:

Source: MS Pluteus 29.1, fol. 109

Source: MS Pluteus 29.1, fol. 109

Institut für Mittelalterliche Musikforschung.

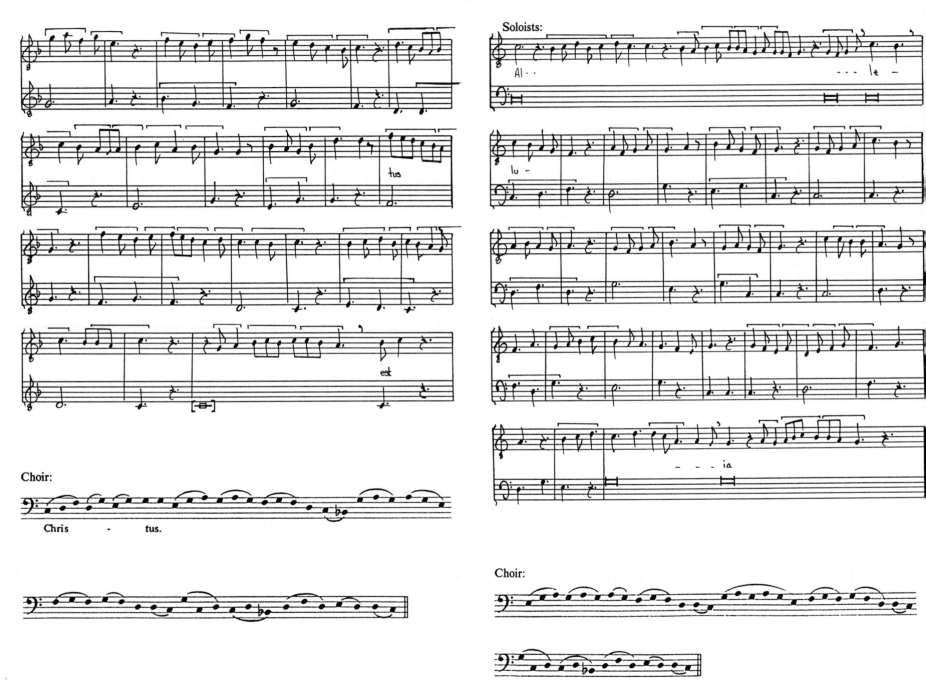

24

Soloists:

Al - - - - le -

lu -

est

tus

- - - ia

Choir:

Chris - tus.

Choir:

14. NOSTRA PHALANS, Versus
Anonymous

Nos- tra pha- lans plau-tat le-ta hic in di- e que oth-le- ta Cris-ti gau-det si-ne me-ta Ja-co-bus in glo-ri- a. An- ge-lo-rum in cu-ri- a.

Nostra phalans plaudat leta
hac in die, qua athleta
Christi gaudet sine meta,
Jacobus in gloria.
Angelorum in curia.

Let our joyful phalanx [or, company] praise
on this day, when the athlete
of Christ rejoices without limit,
James in glory.
In the court of the angels.

Quem Herodes decollavit
et idcirco coronavit
illum Christus et ditavit
in celesti patria.
Angelorum in curia.

Whom Herod beheaded
and for that reason Christ crowned
him and endowed [or, enriched] him
in the celestial homeland.
In the court of the angels.

Cuius corpus tumulatur
et a multis visitatur
et per illud eis datur
salus in Gallecia.
Angelorum in curia.

Whose body is buried
and is visited by many
and, for that, salvation is given
to them in Galicia.
In the court of the angels.

MS Cod. Calixtinus, fol. 185

Ergo festum celebrantes
eius melos decantantes
persolvamus venerantes
dulces laudes Domino.
Angelorum in curia.

Therefore, celebrating his feast,
chanting [or, discanting] melodies,
venerating, let us offer*
sweet praises to the Lord.
In the court of the angels.

*persolvere = to offer as in payment or
fulfillment of a vow

15. CONGAUDEANT CATHOLICI, Conductus
Anonymous

Con- gau- de- ant ca-thho-li- ci, le- ten-tur ci- ves ce- li- ci, di- e i- sta.

MS Cod. Calixtinus, fol. 185

Congaudeant catholici,
letentur cives celici
die ista.

Let catholics rejoice together,
let the citizens of heaven be glad
on this day.

Clerus pulcris carminibus
studeat atque cantibus,
die ista.

Let the clergy devote itself
to beautiful songs and chants,
on this day.

Hec est dies laudabilis
divina luce nobilis,
die ista.

This is the praiseworthy day,
the celebrated divine day,
on this day.

Qua Jacobus palacia
ascendit ad celestia
die ista.

Inasmuch as James ascended
from the palace into heaven
on this day.

Vincens Herodis gladium
accepit vite bravium
die ista.

Herod's sword overcoming [him; i.e., James],
he received the reward of eternal life
on this day.

Ergo carenti termino,
benedicamus domino,
die ista.

Therefore, without ceasing,
let us bless the Lord,
on this day.

Magno patri familias
solvamus laudis gracias,
die ista.

To the great Father of all
let us offer thanks of praise,
on this day.

16. REGNAT, Substitute Clausulae, Anonymous

16a. Source: MS Pluteus 29.1, fol. 168
Institut für Mittelalterliche Musikforschung.

17. ALLELUIA, NATIVITAS, Organum triplum
Pérotin (fl. c. 1190–c. 1225)

Alleluia.

Alleluia.

℣ Nativitas gloriose Virginis Marie
ex semine Abrae orta de tribu Iuda.

℣ The birth of the glorious Virgin Mary,
from the seed of Abraham, risen from
the tribe of Judah.

18. MORS, Organum quadruplum
Pérotin (fl. c. 1190-c. 1225)

Source: MCA MUSIC, A Division of MCA Music, Inc., NY.

Alleluia.

Alleluia.

℣ Christus resurgens ex mortuis
iam non moritur
mors illi ultra non dominabitur.
(Romans 6:9)

℣ Christ rising again from the dead
now dieth not,
death will not have power over him.

Alleluia.

Alleluia.

Veri floris sub figura,
Quem produxit radix pura,
cleri nostri pia cura,
florem fecit mysticum
praeter usum laicum,
sensum trahens tropicum
floris a natura.

Under the figure of the true flower
which the pure root produced,
the loving devotion of our clergy
has made a mystical flower,
extracting an allegorical meaning,
beyond ordinary usage,
from the nature of a flower.

19. VERI FLORIS, Conductus
Anonymous

20. HAC IN ANNI IANUA, Conductus
Anonymous

[Fol. 229'-230]

Hac in anni ianua,
hac in Ianuario,
tendamus ad ardua
virtutum subsidio.
Gaudia sunt mutua,
muto facto vitio.
Reproborum fatua
reprobatur actio.

At this opening of [or, gateway to] the year,
in this January,
let us direct our course toward heaven*
supported by virtue.
The joys are mutual,
vice has been made mute.
The foolish action of reprobates
is condemned.

    *The line has double meaning, stating also let us
    turn to difficult tasks

Anni novi novitas
novam leges afferens,
sequi vetat vetitas,
vetustatem auferens.
Probos probet probitas,
probis proba conferens.
Conteratur pravitas,
probitatem conterens.

The newness of the new year
bringing new laws,
it follows that it vetoes that which was prohibited,
sweeping away old conditions.
Moral integrity examines the evidence,
conferring approval on that which is good.
Let the wicked deeds [or, corrupt practices]
wearing down moral integrity be wiped out.

O felices nuptiae!
O felix humanitas,
cui nubit hodie
filii divinitas,
hinc divine glorie
non decrescit quantitas,
sed ad gradum gratie
nostra crescit parvitas.

O, blessed nuptials!
O, fortunate humanity,
to whom today
the divine Son is joined,
from now on, the magnitude of divine glory
does not decrease,
but to the degree of our grace
our significance increases [our smallness grows].

Nostris lumen tenebris
dat lumen de lumine,
prime culpe funebris
exclusa caligine.
De luce lux celebris
nascitur de virgine,
non carnis illecebris,
sed divino flamine.

The light of lights gives
sight [light] to our blindness [darkness],
having blotted out the darkness
of deadly original sin.
The celebrated light of light
is born of a virgin,
not by carnal seduction,
but by the Holy Spirit [by divine breath].

Carnis circumcisio,
mysterii vacua,
non fuit in filio
par quam nobis congrua
datur demonstratio
tollere superflua,
circumcisio vitio,
hac in anni ianua.

Circumcision of the flesh,
empty of mystery,
was not in the Son
by which fitting example
was given to us
to remove the excess,
pruning away evil,
at this beginning of the year.

21. EN NON DIU – QUANT VOI – EIUS IN ORIENTE, Motet
Anonymous

TRIPLUM:

En non Diu, que que nus die,

quant voi l'herbe vert et le tans cler

et le rosignol chanter,
a donc fine amors me prie
docement d'une joliveté chanter:
"Marions leisse Robim por moi amer!"
Bien me doi adés pener
et chapiau de fleurs porter
por si bele amie,
quant voi la rose espanie
l'herbe vert et le tans cler.

In the name of God, whatever anyone says,

when I see the green grass and the clear skies

and the nightingale singing,
then true love begs me
sweetly to sing joyfully:
"Marion, leave Robin for my love!"
Indeed I must take pains
to wear a chaplet of flowers
for such a beautiful lover,
when I see the rose blooming,
the green grass, and the clear skies.

DUPLUM:

Quant voi la rose espanie
l'herbe vert et le tans clear
et le rosignol chanter,
a donc fine amors m'envie
de joie fere et mener,
car qui n'aime, il ne vit mie.

When I see the rose blooming,
the green grass, and the clear skies,
and the nightingale singing,
then true love inspires me
to be joyful and to pursue,
because whoever does not love, only half lives.

Pour ce se doit on pener
d'avoir amors a amie
et servir et honerer,
qui en joie veut durer.
En non Diu, que que nus die,

Whoever wants joy to last
must take pains
to have Love for a friend
and to serve and honor her.
In the name of God, whatever anyone says,

au cuer mi tient li maus d'amer!

the pangs of love hold my heart!

TENOR:

Eius in oriente

From the east they . . .

22. PUCELETE – JE LANGUIS – DOMINO, Motet
Anonymous

TRIPLUM:

Pucelete
bele et avenant,
joliete,
polie et pleisant,
la sadete,
que je desir tant,
mi fait liés,
jolis, envoisiés
et amant:
N'est en mai
einsi gai
roussignolet chantant.
S'amerai
de cuer entieremant
m'amiete,
la brunete,
jolietement.
Bele amie,
qui ma vie
en vo baillie
avés tenue tant,
je voz cri
merci
en souspirant.

TRIPLUM:

A little maid,
comely and fair,
so pretty,
graceful and pleasing,
the charming little one,
whom I desire so much,
makes me happy,
joyful, light-hearted
and loving;
A nightingale
singing in May
is not so gay.
I will love
my little dark-haired
sweetheart,
joyfully,
with my whole heart.
Fair sweetheart,
you who have
so long had my life
in your power,
sighing,
I cry out to you
for mercy.

DUPLUM:

Je langui[s] des maus d'amours:
Mieuz aim assez, qu'il m'ocie
que nul autre maus;
trop est jolie la mort.
Alegiés moi, douce amie,
ceste maladie,
qu'amours ne m'ocie.

DUPLUM:

I languish with the pain of love:
I prefer that it, rather than
any other malady, kill me;
death is so sweet.
Relieve this illness,
sweet beloved,
so that love does not kill me.

TENOR:

DOMINO

—Anonymous

TENOR:

LORD

—Susan Stakel and Joel Relihan

23. AUCUNS VONT SOUVENT—AMOR QUI COR—KYRIE, Motet
Petrus de Cruce (fl. c. 1270-1300)

This music is reproduced by permission of A–R Editions, Inc. It is taken from *The Montpellier Codex, Part III*, edited by Hans Tischler, published as volumes 6 and 7 of *Recent Researches in the Music of the Middle Ages and Early Renaissance* by A–R Editions, Inc., 801 Deming Way, Madison, WI 53717. Copyright 1978 A–R Editions, Inc.

TRIPLUM:

Aucuns vont souvent
par leur envie mesdisant
d'amours, mes il n'est si bonne vie
com d'amer loiaument;
quar d'amours vient toute courtoisie
et tout honour et tout bon ensegnement.
Tout ce puet en li prouver, qui amie
veut faire sans boisdie
et amer vraiement,
que ja en li n'iert assise vilanie
ne couvoitise d'amasser argent.
Ains aime bonne compaignie
et despent adés largement;

et si n'a en li felonnie
n'envie sus autre gent,
mes a chascun s'umelie
et parole courtoisement.

S'il a du tout sans partie
mis son cuer en amer entierement;
et sachiés, qu'il n'aime mie,

ains ment, s'il se demaine autrement.

DUPLUM:

Amor, qui cor vulnerat
humanum, quem generat
carnalis affectio,
numquam sine vicio
vel raro potest esse,
quoniam est necesse,
ut quo plus diligitur
res, que cito labitur
et transit, eominus
diligatur *Dominus*.

TENOR:

Kyrie

TRIPLUM:

Some often go around
badmouthing love out of envy,
but there is no life so good
as loving loyally;
for from love comes all courtesy
and all honor and all good upbringing.
All of this can be shown by one who
takes a sweetheart without deceit
and loves her truly.
Villainy will never reside in him,
nor will the desire to amass money.
Rather, he loves fair company
and always spends his money
generously;
and there is in him no ill-will
nor envy toward other people,
but he humbles himself
and speaks courteously toward other
people.
If he has wholly, without exception,
set his heart entirely on loving;
and know, that he who conducts himself
otherwise,
does not love at all; rather he lies.

DUPLUM:

Love, which wounds the human heart,
love, which carnal lust
creates,
never or rarely can exist
without sin,
for it must be,
that the more a thing is loved
which quickly decays
and passes away, the less
the Lord is loved.

TENOR:

Lord [have mercy]

24. SUMER IS ICUMEN IN, Rota-Motet
Anonymous

Source: MS Harley 978, fol. 11v, British Museum.

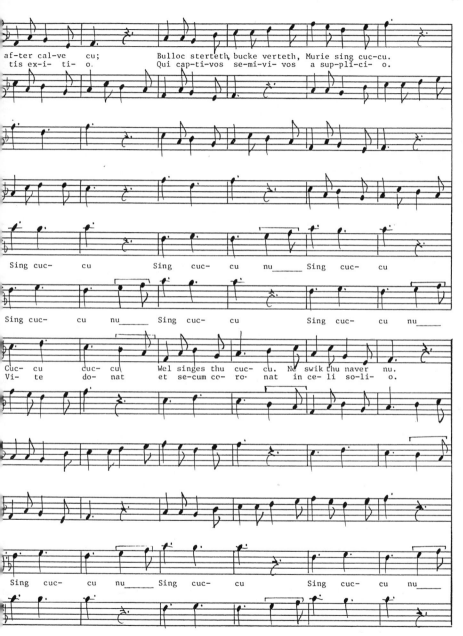

af-ter cal-ve cu; Bulloc sterteth, bucke verteth, Murie sing cuc-cu.
tis ex-i- ti- o. Qui cap-ti-vos se-mi-vi- vos a sup-pli-ci- o.

Sing cuc- cu Sing cuc- cu nu Sing cuc- cu

Sing cuc- cu nu Sing cuc- cu Sing cuc- cu nu

Cuc- cu cuc- cu Wel singes thu cuc- cu. Ne swik thu naver nu.
Vi- te do- nat et se-cum co- ro- nat in ce- li so-li- o.

Sing cuc- cu nu Sing cuc- cu Sing cuc- cu nu

TRIPLUM:

Sumer is icumen in
Lhude sing cuccu.
Groweth sed and bloweth med,
and springth wde nu.
Sing cuccu.
Awe bleteth after lomb,
Lhouth after calve cu,
Bulluc sterteth,
bucke verteth.
Murie sing cuccu.
Cuccu, cuccu.
Wel singes thu cuccu.
Ne swik thu naver nu.

DUPLUM:

Perspice Christicola, que dignatio.
Celicus agricola pro vitis vicio,
Filio non partens exposuit mortis exitio.

Qui captivos semivivos a supplicio
Vite, donat, et secum, coronat, in celi
  solio.

PES:

Sing cuccu nu, Sing cuccu.

Sing cuccu, Sing cuccu nu.

TRIPLUM:

Summer is a-coming in,
Loudly sing, cuckoo.
Groweth seed and bloweth mead,
And springeth the wood anew.
Sing, cuckoo.
The ewe bleats for the lamb,
The cow lows for the calf,
The bullock leaps,
the buck becomes bold.
Merrily sing, cuckoo.
Cuckoo, cuckoo.
You sing well, cuckoo.
Never shall you cease now.

DUPLUM:

Observe, Christians, what an honor!
The heavenly farmer (i.e., Father),
  because of the blemish of the vine,
  not sparing His Son, exposed him to
  the destruction of death.
[He] Who delivers half-alive captives
  from punishment to life, and crowns
  [them] with himself in the heavenly
  throne.

—Duplum translated by Fr. Dick John

PES:

Sing cuckoo now; Sing cuckoo.

Sing cuckoo; Sing cuckoo now.

The manuscript's performance instructions contain no directive for concluding
this piece.

25. Excerpt from ORDO VIRTUTUM, Liturgical Drama
Hildegard von Bingen (1098-1179)

PATRIARCHAE ET PROPHETAE Qui sunt hi, qui ut nu-bes?

VIRTUTES O anti-qui sancti, quid admirami-ni in no-bis? Ver — bum De — i cla-rescit in forma ho-mi-nis, et id-e-o fulge — mus cum il-lo, æ-di-fican-tes membra su-i pul-chri corpo — ris.

PATRIARCHAE ET PROPHETAE Nos sumus radi — ces et vos ra-mi, fructus vi-ven-tis o-culi, et nos um-bra in il-lo fu — i-mus.

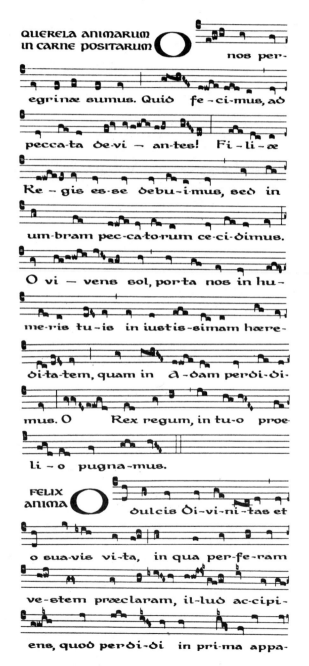

QUERELA ANIMARUM IN CARNE POSITARUM O nos per-egrinæ sumus. Quid fe-ci-mus, ad peccata de-vi — an-tes! Fi-li-æ Re — gis es-se debu-i-mus, sed in um-bram pec-ca-to-rum ce-ci-dimus.

O vi — vens sol, por-ta nos in hu — me-ris tu-is in iustis-simam hære-di-ta-tem, quam in A-dam perdi-di-mus. O Rex regum, in tu-o proe-li — o pugna-mus.

FELIX ANIMA O dulcis Di-vi-ni-tas et o sua-vis vi-ta, in qua per-fe-ram ve-stem præclaram, il-lud ac-cipi-ens, quod perdi-di in pri-ma appa-

ri-ti — one, ad te sus-pi-ro et o-mnes vir-tu-tes in-vo -co.

VIRTUTES O felix a-ni-ma et o dulcis cre-atu — ra De-i, quæ æ-di-fi — ca-ta es in pro-fun-da altitu-di-ne sa-pi-enti-æ De-i, mul — tum a-mas.

FELIX ANIMA O li-benter ve-ni-am ad vos, ut præbe-a-tis mi-hi osculum cor-dis.

VIRTUTES Nos de-bemus mi-li-ta — re tecum, o fi-li-a Re-gis.

SED GRAVATA ANIMA CONQUERITUR O gravis la-bor et o durum pondus, quod habe-

From Hildegard von Bingen: LIEDER, ed. Pudentiana Barth, M. Immaculata Ritscher, and Joseph Schmidt-Gorg (Salzburg, Austria: Otto Muller Verlag, 1969). Used by permission.

40

ta - tem non a - mi - si-sti, et quæ a -

va-ri-ti-am guttu - ris an-ti-qui

serpen -tis i-bi non de - vo -

ra - sti.

DIABOLUS: Quæ est hæc potestas, quod nullus sit præter Deum? Ego autem dico: Qui voluerit me et voluntatem meam sequi, dabo illi omnia. Tu vero tuis sequacibus nihil habes, quod dare possis, quia etiam vos omnes nescitis quid sitis.

HUMILITAS: -go cum me-is so-da-

libus be-ne sci-o, quod tu es il-le

antiquus dra-co, qui su-per sum -

mum vo-la-re vo-lu-i-sti, sed i-pse

Deus in a-bys-sum pro-ie-cit te.

VIRTUTES: -os autem omnes in

excel-sis ha-bi-ta-mus.

HUMILITAS: -go humi-li-tas, re-

gi-na virtu-tum, di-co: Ve-ni-te ad

me, virtu-tes, et enutri-am vos

ad requi-ren-dam perdi-tam drach-

mam et ad co-ro-nan-dum in per-se-

ve-ran-ti-a fe - li-cem.

VIRTUTES: glori-o-sa regi-na

et o sua-vis-si-ma me-di-atrix, li-

ben-ter ve-ni-mus.

HUMILITAS: de-o di-lectis-simæ fi-

li - æ, tene-o vos in rega-li

tha-la-mo.

CARITAS: -go ca-ri-tas, flos a-

ma-bi-lis, ve-ni-te ad me, vir-tu-tes,

et perdu-cam vos in can-di - dam

lucem flo-ris vir - gæ.

VIRTUTES: di-lectis-sime flos,

ardenti desideri-o cur-ri-mus

ad te.

TIMOR DEI: -go timor De-i, vos

fe-licissi-mas fi-li - as præ-pa-

ro, ut in-spi-ci-a-tis in De-um

vi - vum et non pere-a-tis.

VIRTUTES: timor, val-de u-ti-

lis es no-bis, ha-be-mus e-nim

per-fe-ctum stu-di - um numquam

a te se-pa-ra-ri.

PATRIARCHAE ET PROPHETAE:

Qui sunt his, qui ut nubes?

VIRTUTES:

O antiqui sancti, quid admiramini in nobis? Verbum Dei clarescit in forma hominis, et ideo fulgemus cum illo, aedificantes membra sui pulchri corporis.

PATRIARCHAE ET PROPHETAE:

Nos sumus radices et vos rami, fructus viventis oculi, et nos umbra in illo fuimus.

QUERELA ANIMARUM IN CARNE POSITARUM:

O nos peregrinae sumus. Quid fecimus, ad peccata deviantes! Filiae Regis esse debuimus, sed in umbram peccatorum cecidimus. O vivens sol, porta nos in humeris tuis in iustissimam haereditatem, quam in Adam perdidimus. O Rex regum, in tuo proelio pugnamus.

FELIX ANIMA:

O dulcis Divinitas et o suavis vita, in qua perferam vestem praeclaram, illud accipiens, quod perdidi in prima apparitione, ad te suspiro et omnes virtutes invoco.

VIRTUTES:

O felix anima et o dulcis creature Dei, quae aedificata es in profunda altitudine sapientae Dei, multum amas.

FELIX ANIMA:

O libenter veniam ad vos, ut praebeatis mihi osculum cordis.

PATRIARCHS AND PROPHETS:

Who are these, who [are] like clouds?

VIRTUES:

O ancient holy ones, what makes you wonder at us? The Word of God becomes clear [= is made understandable] in the form of a man, and therefore we shine brightly with him, edifying members of his glorious body.

PATRIARCHS AND PROPHETS:

We are the roots and you the branches, fruit of the living bud [= eye], and we were a shadow in him [i.e., a reflection of him].

COMPLAINT OF SOULS PLACED IN FLESH [= bodies]:

O we are pilgrims. What we have done, straying into sins! We ought to be daughters of the King, but we fall into the shadow of sins. O living Sun, carry us on your shoulders into the most equitable inheritance, which, through Adam, we lost. O King of kings, we are fighting in your battle.

FORTUNATE SOUL:

O sweet Divinity and O delightful life, in which I shall wear radiant clothing, receiving that, which I lost in [my] first appearance, to you I sigh and I invoke all virtues.

VIRTUES:

O fortunate soul and O sweet creation of God, you who have been created in the profound height of God's wisdom, you love much [= many things].

FORTUNATE SOUL:

O gladly will I come to you, so that you can offer me the kiss of [your] heart.

VIRTUTES:

Nos debemus militare tecum, o filia Regis.

SED GRAVATA ANIMA CONQUERITUR:

O gravis labor et o durum pondus, quod habeo in veste huius vitae, quia nimis grave mihi est contra carnem pugnare.

VIRTUTES AD ANIMAM ILLAM:

O anima, voluntate Dei constituta, et o felix instrumentum, quare tam debilis es contra hoc, quod Deus contrivit in virginea natura? Tu debes in nobis superare Diabolum.

ANIMA ILLA:

Succurrite mihi adiuvando, ut possim stare.

SCIENTIA DEI AD ANIMAM ILLAM:

Vide quid illud sit, quo es induta, filia salvationis, et esto stabilis et numquam cades.

INFELIX ANIMA:

O nescio quid faciam aut ubi fugiam. O vae mihi, non possum perficere hoc, quo sum induta. Certe illud volo abicere.

VIRTUTES:

O infelix conscientia, o misera anima, quare abscondis faciem tuam coram Creatore tuo?

SCIENTIA DEI:

Tu nescis ned vides nec sapis illum qui te constituit.

ANIMA ILLA:

Deus creavit mundum, non facio illi iniuriam, sed volo uti illo.

VIRTUES:

Our duty is to fight with you, O daughter of the King.

BUT THE TROUBLED SOUL COMPLAINS:

O the arduous labor and O the heavy burden that I have in the clothing of this life, because it is so difficult for me to fight against the flesh.

VIRTUES, TO THAT SOUL:

O soul, created by the will of God, and O fortunate instrument, why are you so troubled against that, which God wiped out in the virgin nature? You must, through us, overcome the Devil.

THAT SOUL:

Hasten to aid me, so that I can stand firm.

KNOWLEDGE OF GOD, TO THAT SOUL:

Consider what it is that you are clothed in, daughter of salvation, and be firm and you will never fail.

UNHAPPY SOUL:

O, I know not what to do or where to flee. O, woe is me, I cannot wear to the end this [garment] in which I am clothed. Certainly, I wish I could cast this off.

VIRTUES:

O unhappy conscience, O wretched soul, why do you hide your face in the presence of your Creator?

KNOWLEDGE OF GOD:

You do not know, neither do you see nor understand the one who created you.

THAT SOUL:

God created the world, I do no harm to that one [= Him], but I want to enjoy it [= the world].

STREPITUS DIABOLI AD ANIMAM ILLAM:

Fatue! fatue! quid prodest tibi laborare? Respice mundum, et amplectetur te magno honore.

VIRTUTES:

O plangens vox est haec maximi doloris. Ach! ach! quaedam mirabilis victoria in mirabili desiderio Dei surrexit, in qua delectatio carnis se latenter abscondit. Heu! heu! ubi voluntas crimina nescivit, et ubi desiderium hominis lasciviam fugit. Luge, luge ergo in his, innocentia, quae in pudore bono integritatem non amisisti, et quae avaritiam gutturis antiqui serpentis ibi non devorasti.

DIABOLUS:

Quae est haec potestas, quod nullis sit praeter Deum? Ego autem dico: Qui voluerit me et voluntatem meam sequi, dabo illi omnia. Tu vero tuis sequacibus nihil habes, quod dare possis, quia etiam vos omnes nescitis quid sitis.

HUMILITAS:

Ego cum meis sodalibus bene scio, quod tu es ille antiquus draco, qui super summum volare voluisti, sed ipse Deus in abyssum proiecit te.

VIRTUTES:

Nos autem omnes in excelsis habitamus.

HUMILITAS:

Ego humilitas, regina virtutum, dico: Venite ad me, virtutes, et enutriam vos ad requirendam perditam drachmam et ad coronandum in perseverantia felicem.

THE LOUD VOICE OF THE DEVIL, TO THAT SOUL:

Foolish! Idiotic! what do you gain by being distressed? Turn your attention to the world, and it will favor you with great honor.

VIRTUES:

O this voice is bewailing of the greatest sorrow. Oh! oh! now a marvelous victory has arisen in the wonderful desire of God, in which delight of the flesh secretly concealed itself. Alas! alas! where the will knew no fault, and where man's desire fled from lust. Grieve, lament therefore in these [things], Innocence, who did not give up [your] integrity in [your] virtuous modesty, and who did not swallow the ancient serpent's gluttonous greed there.

DEVIL:

What is this power, that no one can surpass God? But I say: Whoever is willing to follow me and my will, to that one I will give all things. Truly, you have nothing in your control, that you can give, because none of you know what you are.

HUMILITY:

I, with my companions, know well, that you are that ancient dragon, who wanted to fly above the highest, but God Himself threw you into the abyss.

VIRTUES:

However, we all dwell in the highest [= heaven].

HUMILITY:

I, Humility, queen of the virtues, say: Come to me, Virtues, and I will nourish you to search for the lost drachma [= coin] and to crown the fruitful [one] in persevering [i.e., the fruitful one who persists to the end].

VIRTUTES:

O gloriosa regina et O suavissima mediatrix, libenter venimus.

HUMILITAS:

Ideo, dilectissimae filiae, teneo vos in regali thalamo.

CARITAS:

Ego caritas, flos amabilis, venite ad me, virtutes, et perducam vos in candidam lucem floris virgae.

VIRTUTES:

O dilectissime flos, ardenti desiderio currimus ad te.

TIMOR DEI:

Ego timor Dei, vos felicissimas filias praeparo, ut inspiciatis in Deum vivum et non pereatis.

VIRTUTES:

O timor, valde utilis es nobis, habemus enim perfectum studium numquam a te separari.

—Hildegard von Bingen

VIRTUES:

O glorious queen and O most pleasant mediator, we come willingly.

HUMILITY:

For that, most beloved daughters, I keep you in the royal bed chamber.

CHARITY:

I am Charity, flower worthy to be loved, come to me, Virtues, and I will bring you into the white light of the flower of the branch [i.e., a genealogical branch].

VIRTUES:

O dearest flower, we run to you with burning desire.

FEAR OF GOD:

I, Fear of God, prepare you, most fortunate daughters, so that you may look upon the living God and not perish.

VIRTUES:

O Fear [of God], you are exceedingly useful to us; indeed, we have perfect devotion [= zeal] never to be separated from you.

26. REIS GLORIOS, Chanson
Guiraut de Bornelh (c. 1140–c. 1200)

Reis glorios, verai lums e clartatz,__
Deus poderos, senher, si a vos platz__
Al meu companh sias fizels aiuda,
Qu'eu non la vi____ pos la noitz ton venguda,
Et ades sera l'alba.__

Reis glorios, verai lums e clartatz,	Glorious king, true light and clarity,
Deus poderos, senher, si a vos platz,	God Almighty, Lord, if it pleases Thee,
Al meu companh sias fizels aiuda,	To my companion be a faithful aide,
Qu'eu non la vi pos la noitz ton venguda,	For I have not seen him since night fell,
Et ades sera l'alba.	And soon it will be dawn.

Kalenda maya	The First of May Festival
Ni fuelhs de faya	Neither leaves of beech
Ni chanz d'auzelh	Nor song of birds
Ni flors de glaya	Nor flower of lily [or, iris]
Non es que'm playa,	Are what please me,
Pros domna guaya,	Gracious, joyful lady,
Tro qu'un ysnelh	Until I receive
Messatgier aya	A messenger
Del vostre belh	From your beautiful self,
Cors, que'm retraya	That gives me
Plazer novelh	New pleasure,
Qu'Amors m'atraya,	Which Love brings me,
E jaya E'mtraya	And joy, and I am drawn
Vas vos, Domna veraya;	To you, true lady;
E chaya De playa	And may he die of wounds,
'Lgelos	The jealous one,
Ans que'm n'estraya.	Before I am driven away.

27. KALENDA MAYA, Dansa
Raimbaut de Vaqueiras (d. 1207)

Kalenda maya Ni fuelhs de faya Ni chanz d'auzelh__ Ni flors de glaya
Non es que·m playa, Pros domna guaya, Tro qu'un ysnelh__ Messatgier a·ya Del vostre
belh Cors,que·m retraya Plazer no·velh Qu'Amors m'atraya, E jaya E·m traya Vas
vos, Domna veraya; E chaya De playa·Lgelos Ans que·m n'estraya.__

Breitkopf & Härtel, Wiesbaden. Used by permission.

28. PRENDÉS I GARDE, Rondeau
Guillaume d'Amiens (fl. late 13th century)

Prendés i garde, s'on mi regarde! S'on mi regarde,
dites le moi. C'est tout la jus en cel boschaige:
Prendés i garde, s'on mi regarde. La pastourele
i gardoit vaches: Plaisans brunette a vous m'otroi! Prendés i garde, s'on mi regarde! S'on mi regarde, dites le moi.

Prendés i garde, s'on mi regarde!	Take care that no one looks at me!
S'on mi regarde, dites le moi.	If anyone looks at me, tell me.
C'est tout la jus en cei boschaige:	It is all down there in those woods.
Prendés i garde, s'on mi regarde!	Take care that no one looks at me!
La pastourele i gardoit vaches:	The country girl tends the cows:
Plaisans brunette a vous m'otroi!	Pretty brunette, I am yours!
Prendés i garde, s'on mi regarde!	Take care that no one looks at me!
S'on mi regarde, dites le moi.	If anyone looks at me, tell me.

29. DIEUS SOIT, Ballade with Refrain
Adam de la Halle (c. 1245–c. 1288)

Diex soit en cheste maison,	God be in this house,
Et bien et joie à fuison.	And well-being and joy abundantly.
No sires noueus	Our sovereign lord
Nous envoie à ses amis;	Sends us to his friends;
Ch'est as amoureus	That is, to the enamoured
Et as courtois bien apris,	And to the polite, well-bred [persons],
Pour avoir des pareisis	To have some of paradise
À no hélison.	Have mercy on us.
Nos sires est teus	Our lord is such [a person]
Qu'il prieroit à envis;	That he would pray against the grain [i.e., even when he did not feel like it];
Mais as frans honteus	But to the reluctant [or, disreputable] Franks
Nous a en son lieu tramis,	He sent us in his stead,
Qui sommes de ses nouris	Who are [members] of his family
Et si enfançon.	And as babies.
Diex soit en cheste maison,	God be in this house,
Et bien et joie à fuison.	And well-being and joy abundantly.

—Adam de la Halle

Source: MCA MUSIC, A Division of MCA Music, Inc., NY.

30. A L'ENTRADA DEL TENS CLAR, Ballade
Anonymous

31. OR LA TRUIX, Virelai
Anonymous

A l'entrada del tens clar, Eya,
Pir joie recomençar, Eya,
E pir jalous irritar, Eya,
Vol la regine mostrar
K'ele est si amorouse.
Alavi', alavie,
Jalous, lassaz nos,
lassaz nos ballar entre nos
entre nos.

When the good weather comes, Eya,
to bring back joy, Eya,
and to annoy jealous ones, Eya,
I wish to show the queen
for she is so much in love.
On your way, on your way,
jealous ones, leave us,
leave us to dance among ourselves,
among ourselves.

Or la truix trop asprete, Voir voir!
A ceu k'elle est simplete.
Trop pour outre cuidies me tains
Cant je cuidole estre certains
De ceu loe n'a verai des mois. Oix! Oix!

C'est ceu ke plus me blesce.
Or la truix trop asprete, Voir, voir!
A ceu k'elle est simplete.

I find her much too difficult, indeed!
Because she is so simple.
Much too presumptuous did I act,
Though I felt positively sure
Of what I shall not have for months,
    alas!
'Tis that which hurts me most of all.
I find her much too difficult, indeed!
Because she is so simple.

32. LE JEU DE ROBIN ET DE MARION, "Robins m'aime"
Rondeau
Adam de la Halle (c. 1245-c. 1288)

Robins m'aime, Robins m'a,
Robins m'a demandée, si m'ara.
Robins m'acata cotèle
D'escarlate bone et bèle,
Souskanie et chainturèle,
A leur i va.
Robins m'aime, Robins m'a,
Robins m'a demandée, si m'ara.

Robin loves me, Robin has me,
Robin has asked me, if he will have me.
Robin bought me a robe
Of beautiful, superior quality cloth,*
A smock and a narrow girtle.
For them I consent.**
Robin loves me, Robin has me,
Robin has asked me, if he will have me.

—Adam de la Halle

*escarlate = cloth of superior quality, of various colors; *bone et bele* reenforce the fact that the cloth is good and lovely and of excellent quality.
**A leur i va = an idiomatic expression, ancient form of the modern *Va pour cela!* (literally, I go for that!) meaning I agree, or I consent.

Source: MCA MUSIC, A Division of MCA Music, Inc., NY.

33. A CHANTAR MES AL COR, Trobar
Beatritz, Countess of Dia (born c. 1140)

Lyrics printed with the music in MS fr. 844, folios 204r–204v: Bibliothèque nationale, Paris, France.

A chantar m'es al cor que non deurie.

tant mi rancun cele a qui sui amigs.*

et si l'am mais que nule ren qui sie.

non mi val ren beltat ni curtesie,

ne ma bontaz ne mon pres ne mon sen.

altresi sui enganade et tragide.

qu'eusse fait vers lui desavinence.

—Countess of Dia

It is mine [i.e., my lot] to sing of what I would rather not,

so much bitterness have I toward the one whose lover I am;

for I love her more than anything that exists.

Of no avail to me are [my] virtue [or, good name] or courtly manners,

nor my handsomeness [or, good looks] nor my worth nor my intelligence.

Likewise, I have been deceived and betrayed,

as if I were loathsome to her.

The lyrics usually recorded appear in another French manuscript, without music:

A chantar m'er de so qu'eu no volria

tant me rancur de lui cui sui amia*

Car eu l'am mais que nulha ren que sia

Vas lui no.m val merces ni cortezia

Ni ma beltatz ni mos pretz ni mos sens,

Qu'atressi.m sui enganad' e trahia
Com degr' esser s'eu fos desavinens.

*amigs = a male lover; amia = a female lover

I must sing of that which I would rather not;

I am so aggrieved by him whose lover I am,

for I love him more than anything that be.

Pity and courtliness do not help me with him,

Nor my beauty, nor my worth, nor my intelligence,

For also I am tricked and betrayed
As I would deserve to be if I were loathsome.

34. CANTIGAS DE SANTA MARÍA
Anonymous

a. PORQUE TROBAR, Prologo

Por-que tro - bar é cou-sa en que jaz

en - ten-di - men-to, por-en quen o faz á - o d'a -

ver, et de ra-zon as - saz, per-que en - ten-da et

sa - bia di - zer o que en - tend' e de di - zer lle

praz; ca ben tro - bar as-si s'á de ffa - zer.

Este é o prologo das Cantigas de Santa
Maria, ementando as cousas que á
mester en o trobar.

This is the prologue to the Songs of Holy
[or, Saint] Mary, listing the qualities
that are important for writing verses
[or, composing songs].

Porque trobar é cousa en que jaz,

entendimento, poren quen o faz

áo d'aver, et de razon assaz,

perque entenda et sabia dizer
o que entend' e de dizer lle praz;
ca ben trobar assi s'á de ffazer.

Because composing verse is an art that
requires
understanding, therefore, he who writes
them
must have it, and [also] sufficient
judgment,
to perceive and to know how to say
what he understands and to express it in a
pleasing manner; good verse is composed
in this way.

E macar eu estas duas non ey

com' eu querria, pero provarei
a mostrar ende un pouco que sei,

And though I do not have as much of the
two [understanding and judgment]
as I wish I had,
I will try to show the little that I know,

confiand' en Deus, ond' o saber ven,

ca per ele tenno que poderei
mostrar do que quero algua ren.

trusting in God, from Whom all
knowledge comes
since through Him I think I may be able
to show what I want to [express] in some
way.

b. DES OGE MAIS QUER EU TROBAR, Premeira cantiga de loor

Des o - ge mais quer eu tro - bar pol-a Se -

nnor on - rra - da, en que Deus quis car-ne fi - llar, bẽ -

ey-ta et sa - gra - da, por nos dar gran sol - da -

da no seu rey - no et nos er - dar por seus de sa mas -

na - da de vi - da per - lon - ga - da, sen a - ver -

mos pois a pas - sar per mort' ou - tra ve - ga - da.

Des oge mais quer cu trobar
pola Sennor onrrada,
en que Deus quis carne fillar
bẽeyta et sagrada,
por nos dar gran soldada
no seu reyno et nos erdar
por seus de sa masnada
de vida per longada,
sen avermos pois a passar
per mort' outra vegada.

From today on I want to compose songs
to that honored Lady,
in whom God chose to become flesh,
blessed and holy,
to give us the great reward
of His kingdom and to receive us
as His own with the inheritance
of eternal life,
without us having to pass through
death once again.

a. & b. Adapted from Anglès.

E poren quero começar
  como foy saudada
de Gabriel, u lle chamar
  fóy: "Ben aventurada
  Virgen, de Deus amada,
do que o mund' á de salvar
ficas ora prennada;
e demais ta cunnada*
Elisabeth, que foi dultar,
  é end' envergonnada . . ."

And therefore I want to begin
  as you were greeted
by Gabriel, who announced
  to you: "Most favored
  Virgin, beloved of God,
you now become pregnant with Him
  who is to save the world;
and, moreover, your cousin
Elisabeth, who once doubted,
  now is ashamed . . ."**

*literally, cunnada = sister-in-law;
  however, Elisabeth was Mary's
  cousin.

**Elisabeth is ashamed because she
  doubted the prophecy that she
  would become pregnant.

Additional verses relate to the other Six Joys: the Nativity, Epiphany, Resurrection, Ascension, Pentecost, and Mary's coronation as Queen of Heaven.

35. GLORIA 'N CIELO, Lauda
Anonymous

Ripresa:*
Gloria 'n cielo e pace in terra:
nat' è 'l nostro salvatore.

Refrain:
Glory in heaven and peace on earth:
Born is our Savior.

Nat' è Cristo glorioso,
l'alto Dio maraviglioso;
facto è om desideroso
lo benigno Creatore.

Born is the glorious Christ,
the high marvelous God;
the benign Creator
has made a desirable man.

Della virgine sovrana
rilucente stella diana,
delli erranti tramontana,
puer nato della fiore.

Of the sovereign virgin
a shining morning star,
of the wandering north wind,
a son born of the flower.

Pace 'n terra sia cantata
gloria 'n ciel desiderata;
la donçella consecrata
parturì' à 'l salvatore.

Sing Peace on earth and
desire glory in heaven;
the consecrated maiden
has given birth to the Savior.

*Ripresa is sung at the beginning of the Lauda and at the end of each stanza.

Source: F. Liuzzi, *La Lauda*, n.d.

36. PALÄSTINALIED, Crusade Song
Walter von der Vogelweide (c. 1170-1228)

Nu alerst leb' ich mir werde,

sint myn sündich ouge ersicht.
das here lant und ouch die erde,
dem man vil der eren gicht.

Now for the first time life has meaning
  for me,
since my sinful eyes beheld
the holy land and the very earth
that man honors so much [or, worships
  so much].

Mir ist geschen, als ich ie bat:
ich byn komen an die stat,
die got menslichen trat.

I have seen that for which I prayed:
I have come to the place,
where God walked in human form.

(There are 5 more 7-line stanzas.)

Source: Breitkopf and Härtel, Wiesbaden, Germany.

37. GARRIT GALLUS—IN NOVA FERT—N[EUMA], Motet
Philippe de Vitry (1291-1361)

Philippe de Vitry: *In nova fert-Gallus-N(euma)* taken from "The Roman de Fauvel; The Works of Philippe de Vitry; French Cycles of the *Ordinarium Missae*." *Polyphonic Music of the Fourteenth Century,* Volume I; ed. Leo Schrade, Editions de l'Oiseau-Lyre, Monaco, 1956, pp. 68–70.

TRIPLUM:

Garrit Gallus flendo dolorose

Luget quippe Gallorum concio,

Que satrappe traditur dolose,

Ex cubino sedens officio.
Atque vulpes, tamqual vispilio,
Belial vigens astucia
De leonis consensa proprio
Monarchisat, atat angaria.
Rursus, ecce, Jacob familia
Pharaone altero fugatur;
Non ut olim Iude vestigia
Subintrare potens, lacrimatur.
In deserto fame flagellatur.

Adiutoris carens armatura,
Quamquam clamat, tamen spoliatur,

Continuo forsan moritura.
O miserum exulum vox dura!
O Gallorum garritus doloris,

Cum leonis cecitas obscura

Fraudi paret vulpis proditoris.

Eius fastus sustinens erroris
Insurgito: alias labitur
Et labetur quod habes honoris,
Quod mox in facinis tardis ultoribus
   itur.

TRIPLUM:

The cock [or, Gaul = Frenchman]
   babbles, lamenting sorrowfully,
for, the assembly of cocks [or, Gauls =
   the French nation] mourns,
because it is deceived by the crafty
   satrap,
dutifully sitting in chambers.
And the fox,* like a nocturnal robber,
Belial flourishing with astuteness,
with the consent of the lion** himself,
rules like a monarch. Ah! virtual slavery
Behold, once again, Jacob's family
is put to flight by another pharaoh;
not, as formerly, vestiges being able
to escape into Judah, they weep.
In the desert they are stricken by
   famine.
Lacking the help of arms,
although they cry out, still they are
   robbed;
as a consequence, perhaps they will die.
O harsh voice of the wretched exiles!
O babbling of the mournful cocks [or,
   Gauls = French nation],
since the dark blindness [= lack of
   discernment] of the lion [= the
   King]
is subject to the wrongdoing of the
   traitor fox.
The arrogance of his misdeeds enduring,
rise up in revolt: or what you have
of honor is being and will be lost,
because, if avengers are slow, [people]
   will soon turn to villainy.

*Enguerran de Marigny, who was chief
   councillor to King Philip IV
**the King of France

DUPLUM:

In nova fert animus mutatas
Dicere formas.

Draco nequam quam olim penitus
mirabilis crucis potencia
debellavit Michael inclitus,
Mox Absalon munitus gracia,
Mox Ulixis gaudens facundia
Mox lupinis dentibus armatus,
Sub Tersitis miles milicia,

Rursus vivit in vulpem mutatus,
Cauda cuius, lumine privatus Leo,
Vulpe imperante, paret.
Oves suggit pullis saciatus.

Heu! suggere non cessat et aret.

Ad nupcias carnibus non caret.

Ve pullis mox, ve ceco leoni!

Coram Christo tandem ve draconi.

TENOR:

From the chant Neuma.

DUPLUM:

"My mind is set to tell of bodies
changed into new forms." Ovid:
Metamorphoses, I, 1.
The evil dragon that renowned Michael
once defeated by the power
of the marvelous cross,
Next Absalom endowed with grace,
Next Ulysses's delightful eloquence,
Next, armed with wolfish teeth,
a soldier in military service under
Thersites,
Once more, he lives changed into a fox,
whose tail the Lion, deprived of sight,
obeys, the fox holding political power.
He [i.e., fox] sucks [the blood of] sheep
and is satiated with young chickens.
Alas! he does not cease sucking and
[still] he thirsts.
At wedding feasts he does not abstain
from meats.
Now, woe to the young chickens, woe to
the blind lion!
Finally, in the presence of Christ, woe to
the dragon.

38. DETRACTOR EST — QUI SECUNTUR — VERBUM INIQUUM,
Motet
Philippe de Vitry (1291-1361)

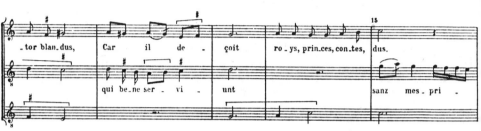

Philippe de Vitry: *Detractor est-Qui Secuntur-Verbum iniquum* taken from "The Roman de Fauvel; The Works of Philippe de Vitry; French Cycles of the *Ordinarium Missae.*" *Polyphonic Music of the Fourteenth Century,* Volume I; ed. Leo Schrade, Editions de l'Oiseau-Lyre, Monaco, 1956, pp. 16–17.

fidelibus qui bene serviunt

sanz mesprison et de vrai cueur seri:

de calice tales bibunt meri.

by the faithful [persons] whom they serve well

without error and with true, kind heart[s]:

from the chalice such [persons] drink pure [wine].

From this point on the text is corrupt.

TENOR:

Verbum iniquum et dolosum
abominabitur Dominus.

TENOR:

An iniquitous and deceitful word will be an abomination to the Lord.

39. MESSE DE NOSTRE DAME, Agnus Dei, Guillaume de Machaut (1300-1377)

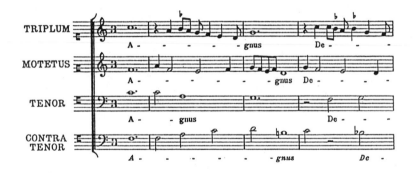

TRIPLUM:

Detractor est nequissima vulpis.
Per ses medis grieve autrui et lui pis,

Sed non minus adulator blandus,
Car il deçoit roys, princes, contes, dus.

Omnibus sunt tales fugiendi,
et li uns plus que li autres, s'endi.

TRIPLUM:

A disparager is the most worthless fox.
Through his slanders [he] harms others and himself worse,
But [he is] no less a bland flatterer,
Because he deceives kings, princes, counts, dukes.
Such [persons] are to be avoided by all, and some more than others.

Much of the remainder of the text is garbled and meaningless, and some of it is corrupt. The main subject continues to be the evil caused by slander and disparagers.

DUPLUM:

Qui secuntur castra sunt miseri,
car pouvrement sont service meri

DUPLUM:

Those who follow camps are wretched, because their services are poorly rewarded

Agnus Dei, qui tollis peccata mundi,
    miserere nobis.
Agnus Dei, qui tollis peccata mundi,
    miserere nobis.
Agnus Dei, qui tollis peccata mundi,
    dona nobis pacem.

Lamb of God, who takest away the sins
    of the world, have mercy on us.
Lamb of God, who takest away the sins
    of the world, have mercy on us.
Lamb of God, who takest away the sins
    of the world, give us peace.

40. MA FIN EST MON COMMENCEMENT, Rondeau
Guillaume de Machaut (1300-1377)

1,4,7 Ma
3 Et
5 Mes

fin te - tiers

est mon
ne u -
chans trois

com - - - - - - men -
re vrai
fois seu -

ce - ment.
e - ment.
le - ment.

82,8 Et mon com - men - ce - ment ma
6 Se re - tro - grade et ein - si

fin.
fin.

Ma fin est mon commencement
et mon commencement ma fin.
Et teneure vraiement.
Ma fin est mon commencement.
Mes tiers fois seulement
se retrograde et einsi fin.
Ma fin est mon commencement
et mon commencement ma fin.

My end is my beginning
and my beginning my end.
And holds indeed.
My end is my beginning.
My third one time only
is retrograde and ends thus.
My end is my beginning
and my beginning my end.

41. QUAM PULCHRA ES, Motet
John Dunstable (c. 1390–1453)

Quam pulchra es et quam decora,
    carissima in deliciis.
Statura tua assimilata est palme,
    et ubera tua botris.
Caput tuum ut Carmelus,
    collum tuum sicut turis eburnea.
Veni, dilecte mi,
    egrediamur in agrum,
et videamus si flores fructus partuierunt,

    si floruerunt mala Punica.
Ibi dabo tibi ubera mea.
    Alleluia.

How beautiful you are and how
    graceful,
    dearest, for allurements.
Your stature is like unto a palm tree,
    and your breasts like the botrys.
Your head is like Carmel,
    your neck like an ivory tower.
Come, my beloved,
    let us go into the field,
and see whether the juice of the flower
    will bear fruit,
    whether the pomegranate trees bud.
There I will give you my loves.
    Alleluia.

—*Biblia Sacra,* Vulgatae, Canticum
    Canticorum IV

42. SALVE, SANCTA PARENS, Carol
Anonymous

BURDEN:

Salve, sancta parens,
enixa puerpera regem.

VERSES:

Salve, porta paradisi,
felix atque fixa,
stella fulgens in sublimi
sidus enixa.

Salve, sancta dominatrix,
Virgo gloriosa,
Virgo imperatrix,
splendens velud rosa.

Salve, virgo benedicta,
mater orphanorum,
deprecamur ut delicta
tergas peccatorum.

BURDEN:

Hail, holy parent,
Mother who gave birth to a king.

VERSES:

Hail, gate of paradise,
blessed and secure,
star shining brightly on high
which gave birth to a constellation.

Hail, holy royal lady,
glorious Virgin,
Virgin empress,
resplendent as a rose.

Hail, blessed Virgin,
mother of orphans,
we beseech you to wipe away
the sins of transgressors.

43. NON AL SUO AMANTE, Madrigal
Jacopo da Bologna (fl. 1340-1360)

Taken from: *The Music of Fourteenth-Century Italy*, edited by Nino Pirrotta (Corpus
Mensurabilis Musicae 8, IV) © 1963 by American Institute of Musicology/Hänssler-Verlag,
Neuhausen-Stuttgart, Germany.

Non al suo amante più Diana piacque
Quando per tal ventura tutto nuda

La vide in mezzo de le gelide acque,
Ch'a me la pastorella alpestra e cruda

Posta a bagnar un leggiadretto velo,
Ch'a l'aura il vago e biondo capel chiuda,
Tal che mi fece, or quand' egli arde 'l cielo,
Tutto tremar d'un amoroso gielo.

Diana did not please her lover more
When by chance he saw her completely nude

In the midst of the icy waters,
Than [pleases] me the rustic and cruel shepherdess

Intent on washing a gossamer veil,
That protects [her] pretty blond hair from the breeze,
So that it makes me, now when the sky burns,
Tremble all over with an amorous chill.

—Francesco Petrarch

44. FENICE FU' E VISSI, Madrigal
Jacopo da Bologna (fl. 1340–1360)

Taken from: *The Music of Fourteenth-Century Italy,* edited by Nino Pirrotta (Corpus Mensurabilis Musicae 8, IV) © 1963 by American Institute of Musicology/Hänssler-Verlag, Neuhausen-Stuttgart, Germany.

Fenice fu' e vissi pura e morbida,

et or son transmutata in una tortora

che vollo con Amor per le bell' ortora.

Arbor secho n' aqua torbida
no' me deleta, may per questo dubito,

va nel' astate l'inverno ven e subito.

Ripresa:

Tal vissi e tal me vivo e posso scrivere
ch' a donna non è più chè honesta
vivere.

—Jacopo da Bologna

I was a phoenix and I lived pure and
    delicate,
and now I am transformed into a
    turtledove
that flies with Love through the
    beautiful orchards.

Dry trees and murky water
do not delight me, but because of this
    doubt,
go in summer, winter comes quickly.

Refrain:

So I lived and so I live and I can write
that for a woman there is no more than
    to live honestly.

45. TOSTO CHE L'ALBA, Caccia
Gherardello da Firenze (c. 1320-c. 1362)

¹A in MS.

Originally published by W. Thomas Marroco, ed., *Fourteenth Century Italian Cacce,* 2nd ed., revised, Medieval Academy of America Publication No. 39 (Cambridge, Mass., 1961), pp. 93–95.

Tosto che l'alba del bel giorno appare

Isveglia li cacciator:
"Su, su, su, su, ch' egli è tempo!"
Alletta li can, te, te, te, te,

Viola, te, Primera, te!"
Su alto al monte con buon cani al mano

E gli bracchetti al piano,
E nella piaggia ad ordine ciascuno.
Io veggio sentir uno de' nostri miglior bracchi.

As soon as the dawn of the beautiful day appears
the hunters arise:
"Up, up, get up! for it is time!
Call out the dogs, You, You [or, "Here, here"],
You, Viola! You, Primera!"
Up high on the mountain with good dogs at hand
and the hounds quiet,
and on the field everyone in order.
I see one of our best hounds scenting.

Starà avvisato.
"Bussate d'ogni lato ciascun

le macchie che Quaglina suona!"
"Ai-o, ai-o!" A te la cerbia viene.

Carbona la prese in bocha la tene.

Ritornello:

Del monte que che v'era su gridava

al altra da l'altra e suo corno sonava.

"Stand alert!"
"Let each one beat the bushes on all
      sides
for the quail calls!"
"Ayo, ayo!" The young doe is coming to
      you.
Carbon has seized her and holds her in
      [his] mouth.

Ritornello:

From the mountain that one who was
      there shouted
to one and to another and sounded his
      horn.

46. SÌ DOLCE NON SONÒ, Madrigal
Francesco Landini (1325-1397)

From Francesco Landini: *Sì dolce non sono,* madrigal taken from The Works of Francesco
Landini, *Polyphonic Music of the Fourteenth Century,* vol. IV ed. Leo Schrade, Editions de
l'Oiseau Lyre Monaco 1974 —pp. 210/212.

1. Sì dolce non sonò chol lir' Orfeo

   Quand' à se trasse fer' uciell' e boschi
   D'amor cantando d'infante di deo.

2. Come lo ghallo mio di fuor da boschi
   Con nota tale che gia ma' udita
   Non fu da Filomena 'n verdi boschi.

3. Ne più Febo cantò quando schernita

   Da Marsia fu suo tibia in folti boschi
   Dove, vincendo, lo spoglio di vita.

Ritornello:

Di Teb' avanc' al chiudent' Anfione

E fecto fa contrario del Gorgone.

Orpheus with his lyre did not sound so sweet
When he drew toward himself wild beasts, birds, and woods,
Singing of love, of childhood, of God.

As [did] my rooster from out of the woods
With such sound as never was heard
From Philomen in the green woods.

No more did Phoebus play when his flute was scorned
By Marsyas in the thick woods
Where, victorious, he [i.e., Phoebus] deprived him [Marsyas] of life.

Ritornello:

Amphion came to Thebes with the purpose of enclosing it
And acted in a manner contrary to that of the Gorgons.*

*Amphion's music caused the stones to move to build the enclosing wall; the Gorgons caused anyone who looked at them to turn to stone.

47. NON AVRÀ MA' PIETÀ, Ballata
Francesco Landini (1325-1397)

Francesco Landini: *Ballata "Non avrà ma' pietà"* taken from "The Works of Francesco Landini,"
Polyphonic Music of the Fourteenth Century, Volume IV; ed. Leo Schrade, Éditions de l'Oiseau-
Lyre, Monaco, 1958, pp. 144–5.

1. Non avrà ma' pietà questa mie
   donna,
   Se tu non faj, amore,
   Ch'ella sia certa del mio grande
   ardore.

This lady of mine will never have mercy,

if you do not see to it, love,
that she is certain of my great ardor.

2. S'ella sapesse quanta pena i' porto

   Per onestà celata nella mente

If she was aware of how much pain I
   bear—
Out of fairness, hidden in my mind—

3. Sol per la sua bellecça, chè conforto
   D'altro non prende l'anima dolente,

only for her beauty, because nothing else
gives comfort to the mournful soul,

4. Forse da lej sarebbono in me spente

   Le fiamme che la pare
   Di giorno in giorno acrescono'l
   dolore.

Perhaps by her there would be
   extinguished in me
the flame that seems
daily to increase pain in her.

5. Non avrà ma' pietà questa mie
   donna,
   Se tu non faj, amore,
   Ch'ella sia certa del mio grande
   ardore.

This lady of mine will never have mercy,

if you do not see to it, love,
that she is certain of my great ardor.

—B. d'Alessio Donati

48. VERGENE BELLA
Guillaume Du Fay (c. 1400–1474)

By American Institute of Musicology/Hänssler-Verlag, D-73762 Neuhausen-Stuttgart, Germany.
Reprinted by permission.

A) Vergene bella, che di sol vestita,

Choronata di stelle al sommo sole

Piacesti, sì, che'n te sua luce ascose;
Amor mi spigne a dir di te parole:

Ma non so'ncominzar senza tu aita,

E di colui ch' amando in te si pose.

B) Invoco lei che ben sempre ripose
Chi la chiamò con fede.
Vergene, s' a mercede
Miseria estrema dell' humane chose
Già mai ti volse, al mio prego t'
inchina.
Soccorri alla mia guerra.

C) Bench' i' sia terra, e tu del ciel
reina.

—from Canzona CCCLXVI,
F. Petrarch

Beautiful Virgin, who, clothed by the
sun,
crowned with stars, so pleased the
highest Sun
that he hid his light in you;
Love impels me to say [these] words to
you:
But I cannot [literally, I do not know
how to] begin without your aid,
and [that] of that One who lovingly
rested within you.

I invoke her who has always answered
whomever called her with faith.
Virgin, if extreme wretchedness
of human affairs ever moved you
to mercy, incline [your ear] to my
prayer.
Uphold [or, help] me in my struggle.

Though I am earth [or, clay], and you
[are] queen of heaven.

49. SE LA FACE AY PALE, Ballade
Guillaume Du Fay (c. 1400-1474)

50. NUPER ROSARUM FLORES — TERRIBILIS EST LOCUS ISTE, Motet
Guillaume Du Fay (c. 1400–1474)

Chant, LU, 1250, basis for motet Tenors:

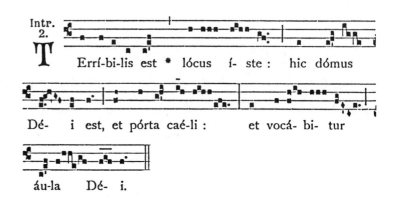

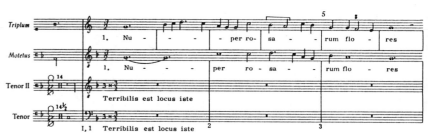

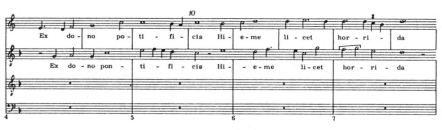

Se la face ay pale	If the [i.e., my] face is pale,
La cause est amer.	the cause is love.
C'est la principale,	It is the principal [reason],
Et tant m'est amer	and it is so bitter for me
Amer, qu'en la mer	to love, that I would rather
Ne voudroye voir;	see myself in the sea [i.e., drown];
Or, scet bien de voir,	Now, she can clearly see,
La belle a qui suis,	the beautiful [lady] whose I am,
Que nul bien avoir	that I cannot have any good [or, good thing]
Sans elle ne puis.	without her.
Se ay pesante malle	If I have a heavy burden
De dueil a porter,	of grief to bear,
Ceste amour est male	this love is hard
Pour moy de porter;	for me to endure;
Car soy deporter	Because she does not want
Ne veult devouloir,	me to have any will
Fors qu'a son vouloir	other than to obey
Obeisse, et puis	her will, and since
Qu'elle a tel pooir,	she has such power,
Sans elle ne puis.	without her I cannot [help myself].
C'est la plus reale	She is the most royal [lady]
Qu'on puist regarder,	that one could consider [or, find].
De s'amour leiale	I cannot keep myself
Ne me puis guarder,	from loving her loyally.
Fol sui de agarder	I am mad to consider
Ne faire devoir	not serving [her],
D'amours recevoir	[and to consider] receiving love
Fors d'elle, je cuij;	elsewhere, I realize;
Se ne veil douloir,	Although I do not want sorrow,
Sans elle ne puis.	without her I am unable [to do anything].

68

Igitur, alma parens	Therefore, gracious parent
Nati tui et filia,	and, at the same time, daughter of your son,
Virgo decus virginum,	Virgin, glory of virgins,
Tuus te FLORENTIAE	your devoted people of Florence
Devotus orat populus,	pray that those who entreat [or, pray]
Ut qui mente et corpore	with a pure mind and heart
Mundo quicquam exorarit.	may obtain whatever they pray for.
Oratione tua	O crucified One,
Cruciatus et meritis	by your prayer and merits
Tui secundum carnem	may your children
Nati domini sui	born according to the flesh
Grata beneficia	be worthy to receive
Veniamque reatum	gracious benefits and remission of sins
Accipere mereatur.	from the Lord.
Amen.	Amen.

TENOR: Terribilis est locus iste   TENOR: Awesome [or, terrible] is this place

Nuper rosarum flores	May the roses recently [received]
Ex dono pontificis	as gift of the Pope
Hieme licet horrida	perpetually decorate,
Tibi, virgo coelica,	even in harsh winter,
Pie et sancte deditum	this grandly constructed temple
Grandis templum machinae	respectfully and solemnly dedicated
Condecorarunt perpetim.	to you, heavenly Virgin.
Hodie vicarius	Today, the vicar
Jesu Christi et Petri	of Jesus Christ, and the successor
Successor EUGENIUS	to Peter, EUGENE,
Hoc idem amplissimum	has seen fit to consecrate
Sacris templum manibus	this most spacious temple
Sanctisque liquoribus	with his sacred hands
Consecrare dignatus est.	and with holy water.

51. MISSA L'HOMME ARMÉ, Agnus Dei
Guillaume Du Fay (c. 1400-1474)

By American Institute of Musicology/Hänssler-Verlag, D-73762 Neuhausen-Stuttgart, Germany.
Reprinted by permission.

(1) *Canon: Cancer eat plenus sed redeat medius.*

Agnus Dei, qui tollis peccata mundi:
miserere nobis.
Agnus Dei, qui tollis peccata mundi:
miserere nobis.
Agnus Dei, qui tollis peccata mundi:
dona nobis pacem.

Lamb of God, who takes away the sins
of the world: have mercy on us.
Lamb of God, who takes away the sins
of the world: have mercy on us.
Lamb of God, who takes away the sins
of the world: give us peace.

52. DE PLUS EN PLUS, Chanson
Binchois (Gilles de Binche; c. 1400-1460)

1. De plus en plus se renouvelle,
   Ma doulce dame gente et belle,
   Ma volonté de vous veir.

   More and more is renewed,
   my sweet lady, noble and beautiful,
   my will to see you.

2. Ce me fait le tres grant desir
   Que j'ay de vous ouir nouvelle.

   This gives me the very great desire
   that I have to hear news of you.

3. Ne cuidiés pas que je recelle,
   Comme a tous jours vous estes celle
   Que je vueil de tout obeir.

   Do not think that I hold back,
   As always you are the one
   whom I want to obey completely.

4. De plus en plus se renouvelle,
   Ma doulce dame gente et belle,
   Ma volonté de vous veir.

   More and more is renewed,
   my sweet lady, noble and beautiful,
   my will to see you.

5. Helas, se vous m'estes cruelle,
   J'auroie au cuer angoisse telle
   Que je voudroie bien morir.

   Alas, if you are cruel to me,
   I shall have such anguish in my heart
   that I would be willing to die.

6. Mais ce seroit sans desservir,

   En soustenant vostre querelle.

   But this would be without disservice [to
   you],
   in upholding your cause.

7. De plus en plus se renouvelle,
   Ma doulce dame gente et belle,
   Ma volonté de vous veir.

   More and more is renewed,
   my sweet lady, noble and beautiful,
   my will to see you.

53. MISSA PROLATIONUM, Kyrie
Johannes Ockeghem (c. 1410-1497)

Kyrie eleison.
Christe eleison.
Kyrie eleison.

Lord, have mercy.
Christ, have mercy.
Lord, have mercy.

54. PARCE, DOMINE, Motet
Jacob Obrecht (c. 1450–1505)

Parce, Domine, populo tuo,
quia pius es et misericors.
Exaudi nos, in aeternum, Domine.

Have mercy, Lord, on your people,
for you are kind and merciful.
Hear us, for ever, Lord.

Source: Glareanus, transcribed from Dodekachordon (published Basle, 1547), p. 260.

55. AVE MARIA, Motet
Josquin Desprez (c. 1440–1521)

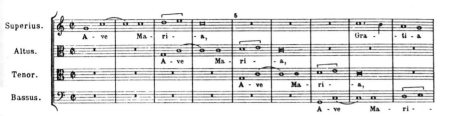

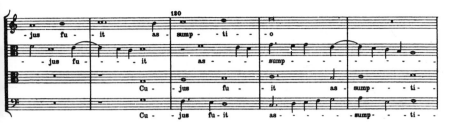

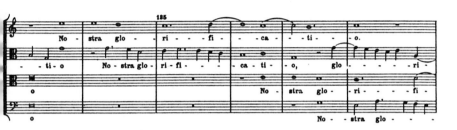

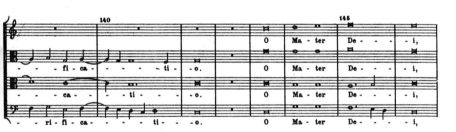

Ave Maria, gratia plena,
Dominus tecum, Virgo serena.

Ave cujus conceptio,
Solemni plena gaudio,
Coelestia, terrestria,
Nova replet laetitia.

Ave cujus nativitas,
Nostra fuit solemnitas,
Ut lucifer lux oriens
Verum solem praeveniens.

Ave pia humilitas
Sine viro foecunditas
Cujus annunciatio
Nostra fuit salvatio.

Ave vera virginitas,
Immaculata castitas,
Cujus purificatio
Nostra fuit purgatio.

Ave praeclara omnibus
Angelicis virtutibus,
Cujus fuit assumptio
Nostra glorificatio.

O Mater Dei
Memento mei.
Amen.

Hail, Mary, full of grace,
The Lord be with you, fair Virgin.

Hail [to you] whose conception,
full of solemn joy,
fills heavenly [and] earthly beings
with new gladness.

Hail [to you] whose nativity,
was our solemn feast,
indeed [was] the morning star rising
preceding the true sun.

Hail, holy humility,
fruitful without man,
whose annunciation
was our salvation.

Hail, true virginity,
undefiled chastity,
whose purification
was our cleansing.

Hail [to you], admirable in all
angelic virtues,
whose assumption was
our glorification.

O, Mother of God,
remember me.
Amen.

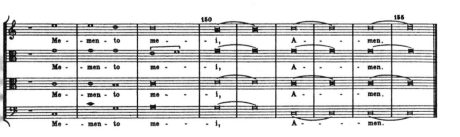

56. ABSALON, FILI MI, Motet*
Josquin Desprez (c. 1440–1521)

*Recorded a tritone higher.

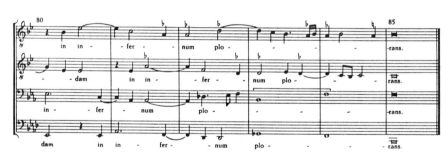

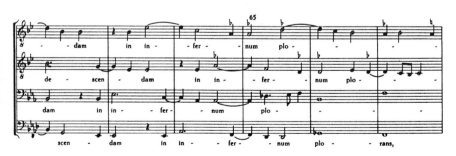

Absalon, fili mi,
fili mi, fili mi, Absalon . . .

Quis det
ut moriar pro te,
fili mi, Absalon?
Non vivam ultra,
sed descendam in infernum plorans.

Absalom, my son,
my son, my son, Absalom . . .

Who will grant
that I may die for you,
my son, Absalom?
Let me not live longer,
but let me descend into hell, weeping.

57. ZWISCHEN PERG UND TIEFFEM TAL, Lied
Heinrich Isaac (c. 1450–1517)

Denkmäler der Tonkunst in Österreich 28, Akademische Druck-u. Verlagsanstalt, Zwischen Perg und Tiefem Tal, Lied by Heinrich Isaac (c. 1450–1517). Reprinted by permission.

Zwischen perg und tieffem tal	Between the mountain and the deep valley
Da ligt ein freie strassen.	There lies a free highway.
Wer seinen půll nit haben mag,	Whoever does not wish to keep his love,
der můss yn faren lassen.	Must let him travel.
Far hin, far hin! Du hast die wal.	Travel there, travel there! You have the choice.
Ich kan mich dein wol massen.	I can measure your welfare myself.
Im jar sind noch vil langer tag,	In a year the day will be much longer still,
Glück ist in allen gassen.	Good fortune is in all paths.

58. SUPER FLUMINA BABYLONIS, Motet
Nicolas Gombert (c. 1495–c. 1560)

By American Institute of Musicology/Hänssler-Verlag, D-73762 Neuhausen-Stuttgart, Germany. Reprinted by permission.

Super flumina Babylonis,	By the waters of Babylon,
illic sedimus et flevimus	there we sat down and wept
dum recordaremur tui, Sion.	when we remembered you, Zion.
In salicibus in medio ejus,	On the willows in the midst thereof,
suspendimus organa nostra;	we hung our instruments [harps];
quia illic interrogaverunt nos,	for there they who have taken us
qui captivos duxerunt nos,	captive asked us,
verba cantionum;	the words of [our] songs;
et qui abduxerunt nos:	and they who have abducted us [said]:
"Hymnum cantate nobis de canticis	"Sing for us a hymn from the songs of
Sion."	Zion."
Quomodo cantabimus canticum Domini	How shall we sing the Lord's song
in terra aliena?	in a strange land?

—Text based on Biblia Sacra, Ps. 136:1–4

59. VICTIMAE PASCHALI LAUDES, Motet
Adrian Willaert (c. 1490–1562)

[Prima Pars]

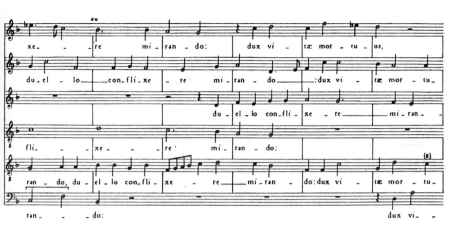

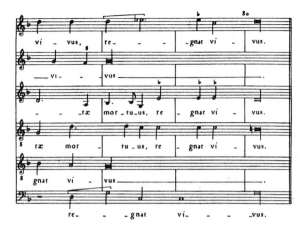

Victimae paschali laudes immolent
   Christiani.
Agnus redemit oves: Christus innocens
   Patri reconciliavit peccatores.

Mors et vita duello conflixere mirando:
   dux vitae mortuus, regnat vivus.

To the Paschal Victim let Christians offer
   songs of praise.
The Lamb has redeemed the sheep:
   sinless Christ has reconciled sinners to
   the Father.

Death and life have clashed in a
   miraculous combat: the leader of life
   died, [yet] living, he reigns.

60. EMENDEMUS IN MELIUS, Motet
Cristóbal de Morales (c. 1500-1553)

From *Complete Works of Morales* by Institute of Musicology/Hänssler-Verlag, D-73762
Neuhausen-Stuttgart, Germany. Reprinted by permission.

88

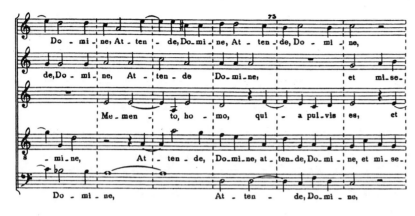

Emendemus in melius quae ignoranter
peccavimus: ne subito praeoccupati,
die mortis, quaeramus spatium
paenitentiae, et invenire non
possimus.

Attende, Domine, et miserere: quia
peccavimus tibi.

ALTO II:
Memento homo, quia pulvis es, et in
pulverem reverteris.

—(Alto II adapted from Biblia
Sacra, Genesis 3:19)

Let us make amends because, in
ignorance, we have sinned: not
anticipating, suddenly, on the day of
death, we may seek a place of
repentance, and not be able to find
[one].

Hear [us], Lord, and have mercy:
because we have sinned against You.

ALTO II:
Remember, man, that you are dust, and
to dust you shall return.

61. OIMÈ EL CUOR, Frottola
Marco Cara (c. 1470–c. 1525)

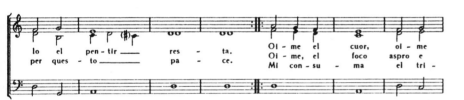

Oimè el cuor! — Alas, my heart!
Oimè la testa! — Alas, my head!
Chi non ama non intenda. — Whoever does not love does not understand.

Oimè Dio, — Alas, God,
che error fece io! — what a mistake I made!
Chi non falla non s'amenda. — Whoever does not sin needs not repent.

Oimè Dio, — Alas, God,
che'l pentir mio! — how I regret it!
Ad amar un cor fallace. — Having catered [or, given in] to a sinful heart.

Dopo il fallo el pentir resta, — After sinning, it remains to repent,
non mi da per questo pace. — for this reason I am given no peace.

Oimè el cuor, oimè la testa. — Alas, my heart; alas, my head.
Oimè, el foco aspro e vivace, — Alas, the fire, harsh and quick,
mi consuma el tristo core. — consumes my sad heart.

Chi non ama non intenda, — Whoever does not love does not understand,
Chi non ama non intenda. — whoever does not love does not understand.

Oimè Dio che'l fatto errore, — Alas, God, what a mistake I have made,
l'alma afflicta, mi molesta. — my aggrieved spirit disturbs me.

62. QUANDO RITROVO LA MIA PASTORELLA, Madrigal
Costanzo Festa (c. 1480–1545)

Taken from: *Costanzo Festa-Collected Works,* edited by Albert Seay (Corpus Mensurabilis Musicae 25, VIII) © 1978 by American Institute of Musicology/Hänssler-Verlag, Neuhausen-Stuttgart, Germany.

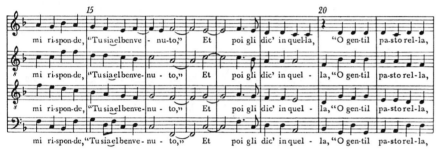

Quando ritrovo la mia pastorella
Al prato con le pecor' in pastura,

Io mi gli accost' e presto la saluto.
La mi risponde, "Tu sia el benvenuto."
E poi gli dic' in quella,
"O gentil pastorella,
Non men crudel che bella,
Sei del mio ben ribella.
Deh non esser ver me cotanto dura."
Cosi rispond' anch' ella,
"Disposta son a quel tuo cordesia,
Ma se non hai denari, va alla tua via.

Ma se non hai denari, va alla tua via."

When I find my shepherdess
In the meadow, with the sheep in the pasture,

I approach her and quickly I greet her.
She answers me, "You are welcome."
And then I say to her,
"O gentle shepherdess,
No less cruel than beautiful,
You fight against my happiness.
Alas! Do not be so harsh to me."
She answers me thus,
"I am [well] disposed to your suit,
But if you do not have money, go on your way.

But if you do not have money, go on your way."

63. DA LE BELLE CONTRADE D'ORIENTE, Madrigal
Ciprano de Rore (1516–1565)

From *Complete Works of Rore,* Vol. 5, 1971 by American Institute of Musicology/Hänssler-Verlag, D-73762 Neuhausen-Stuttgart, Germany. Reprinted by permission.

Da le belle contrade d'oriente
Chiara e lieta s'ergea Ciprigna, et io
Fruiva in braccio al divin idol mio

Quel piacer che non cape humana mente,
Quando sentii dopo un sospir ardente:
Speranza del mio cor, dolce desio
Te'n vai, haime, sola mi lasci, adio.

Che sarà qui di me scura e dolente?

Ahi, crudo Amor, ben son dubiose e corte
Le tue dolcezze, poich' ancor ti godi
Che l'estremo piacer finisca in pianto.

Nè potendo dir più, cinseme forte, cinseme forte,
Iterando gl' amplessi, iterando gl' amplessi, in tanti nodi,
Che giamai ne fer più l'edra o l'acanto.

From the fair regions of the east
Dawn rose, clear and glad, and I,
In the arms of my divine idol, was enjoying

That pleasure which no human mind can comprehend,
When I heard, after an ardent sigh:
"Hope of my heart, sweet desire,
You are going, alas! You are leaving me alone. Farewell!

What will become of me, gloomy and sad?

Ah, cruel Love! Uncertain and short are

Your sweetnesses, for you even rejoice
That the utmost pleasure should end in tears."
Unable to say more, she embraced me strongly, held me fast,
Repeating the embraces, repeating the hugs, in so many entwinings,*
That never either ivy or acanthus made more.

*Literally, in so many knots

64. SOLO E PENSOSO, Madrigal
Luca Marenzio (c. 1553–1599)

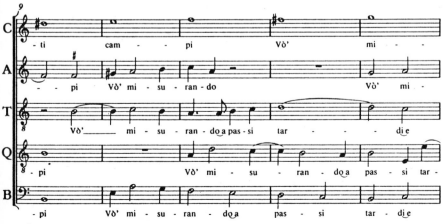

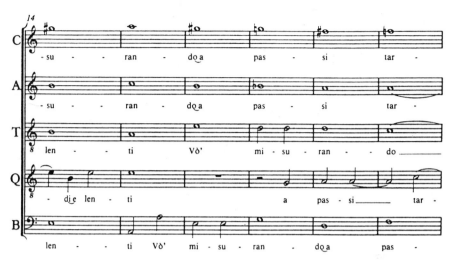

Reprinted by permission of Cambridge University Press, New York, NY.

Solo e pensoso i più deserti campi

Vo' misurando a passi tardi e lenti,
E gli occhi porto per fuggire intenti

Dove vestiggio uman l'arena stampi.

Altro schermo non trovo che mi scampi

Dal manifesto accorger de le genti;
Perchè ne gli atti d' allegrezza spenti
Di fuor si legge com' io dentro avampi:

Sì ch' io mi credo omai che monti e piagge
E fiumi e selve sappian di che tempre

Sia la mia vita, ch' è celata altrui.

Ma pur sì aspre vie ne sì selvagge

Cercar non sò ch' Amor non venga sempre
Ragionando con meco, et io con lui.

—Petrarch

Alone and thoughtful, with lagging and slow steps
I pace the most deserted fields,
and I keep my eyes watchful in order to take flight
whenever human traces mark the earth.

I do not find any other shield that protects me
from the knowing looks of the people;
Because by my actions, drained of joy,
one reads from outside how I burn inside:

So that I now believe that mountains and shore
and rivers and forests know of what temper
my life is, that is hidden from others.

But yet I do not know how to seek pathways
so harsh or so wild that Love does not always
come for the purpose of reasoning with me, and I with him.

65. MORO, LASSO, AL MIO DESOLO, Madrigal
Carlo Gesualdo (c. 1561-1613)

Source: Ugrino Verlag, Hamburg.

Moro, lasso, al mio duolo
E chi mi può dar vita,

Ahi, che m'ancide e non vuol darmi aita!

O dolorosa sorte,
Chi dar vita mi può, ahi, mi dà morte!

I am dying, wretched, in my grief,
And [the one] who is able to give me life,

Alas, is killing me and is not willing to give me aid!

O painful fate,
[The one] who is able to give me life, alas, gives me death!

66. SING WE AND CHANT IT, Ballett
Thomas Morley (c. 1557-1602)

The words of the second stanza must not be sung until the *entire* ballett, with repeats, has been sung to the words of the first stanza.

67. NON È SÌ DENSO VELO, Madrigal
Giaches de Wert (1535–1596)

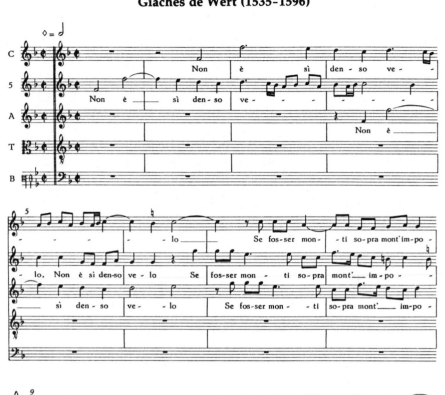

Taken from: *Giaches de Wert—Collected Works,* edited by Carol MacClintock assisted by Melvin Bernstein (Corpus Mensurabilis Musicae 24, VIII) © 1968 by American Institute of Musicology/ Hänssler-Verlag, Neuhausen-Stuttgart, Germany.

Non è sì denso velo
Se fosser monti sopra mont' imposti,
Nè sì remoto cielo,
Che possa far nascosti
E lontan quei bei lumi,
Che nè mari nè fiumi,
Nè paese longinqui,
Faran giamai che non mi sian propinqui.
I' gl' ho s'affissi a gl' occhi
Ch' ogni sguardo ch' io scocchi
Parmi che quel splendor mi senda il viso
Ch' in vita mi mantien, poichè m' ha
    ucciso.

There is no veil so dense
not even mountains piled on mountains,
nor is heaven so remote and far away,
that it could hide
those beautiful eyes [from me],
which neither seas nor rivers,
nor distant lands,
will ever cause not to be near to me.
I have stared into them so intensely
that it seems to me that wherever I look
their splendor comes into my face,
which keeps me alive, after having slain
    me.

68. À CE JOLY MOYS DE MAY, Chanson
Clément Janequin (c. 1485–1558)

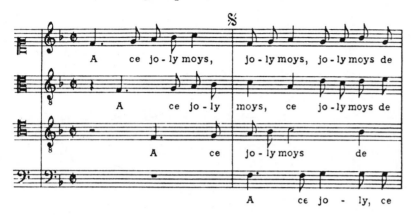

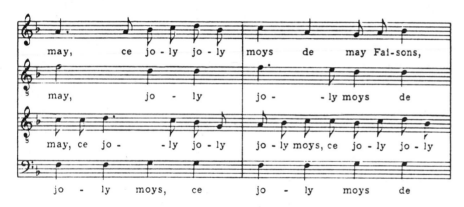

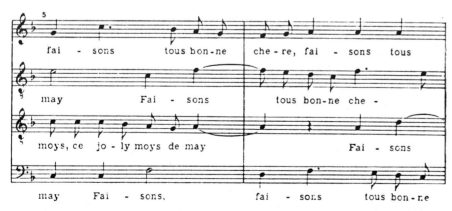

Taken from Clément Janequin: *Chansons Polyphoniques,* Volume III; ed. A. Tillman Merritt and François Lesure, Éditions de l'Oiseau-Lyre, Monaco, 2nd revised edition, 1983, pp. 102–4.

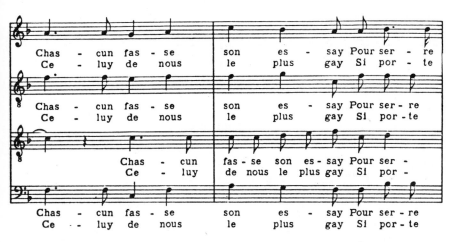

À ce joly moys, ce joly moys de may,
Faisons tous bonne chere.

In this pretty month, this pretty month of May,
Let us live very well!

1. Resveillons nous, ne dormons plus
Dansons, ballons, et au surplus,

Let us wake up, let us sleep no longer,
Let us dance, let us dance [or, have a ball], and, besides,

Chascun fasse son essay
Pour serre la croupiere.

Let each one make his attempt
to tighten the crupper.

Refrain:

Refrain:

À ce joly moys, ce joly moys de may,
Faisons tous bonne chere.

In this pretty month, this pretty month of May,
Let us live very well!

2. À bien pousser n'ayons vains cueurs

To really incite [or, push], let us not have vain hearts.

Donnons dedans soyons vainceurs,
Celuy de nous de plus gay
Si porte la banniere.

Let us look within; let us be conquerors;
That one of us [who is] the liveliest
indeed, carries the banner [or, flag].

Refrain:

Refrain:

À ce joly moys, ce joly moys de may,
Faisons tous bonne chere.

In this pretty month, this pretty month of May,
Let us live very well!

69. Excerpt from REVECY VENIR DU PRINTEMPS,
Musique mesurée
Claude Le Jeune (c. 1530-1600)

Rechant à 5.

Chant à 2.

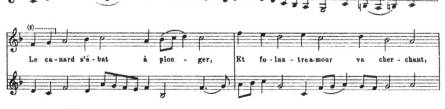

Repeat: Rechant à 5

Chant à 3

Repeat: Rechant à 5

From *Complete Works of Le Jeune,* Volume I, 1952 by American Institute of Musicology/Hänssler-Verlag, D-73762 Neuhausen-Stuttgart, Germany. Reprinted by permission.

RÉCHANT à 5.

Revoicy venir du printemps
L' amoureus le dous et beau temps.

CHANT à 2.

Le superbe cours du torrent

A repris le lit de ses bors,
De la mer le flot tougrondant
Ja toucalme et coy ne sort hors.
Le canard s'ebat à plonger,
Et folastre amour va cherchant,
Ja la grue a fait alonger
sa bataille à pointe fourchant.

RÉCHANT à 5, as before.

CHANT à 3.

Le soleil plu' beau se fait voir
Plu' serain, plu' clair, plu' vermeil,
Le nuage épais se voit choir
Dissipé du ray du grand oeil.

Mille bois de verd se font pleins,
Mille champs de verd se sont peins,
Mille prés De fleurs bigarrés.

RÉCHANT à 5, as before.

The original Old French text, as printed in 1603, is:

REFRAIN:

Revecy venir du Printans
L'amoureuz' et belle saizon.

Le courant des eaus recherchant
Le canal d'été s'éclaircit:
Et la mer calme de ces flots
Amolit le triste courrous:

Le canard s'egaye plonjant,
Et se lave coint dedans l'eau:
Et la gru' qui fourche son vol
Retraverse l'air et s'en va.

REFRAIN: Revecy, etc.

REFRAIN, for 5 voices.

Here comes spring again
the lovely, sweet, and beautiful season.

VERSE, for 2 voices.

The superb course of the torrent
    [= river]
has again filled its bed;
The all-raging mass of the sea
is now tranquil and does not flood.
The duck frolics to dive,
and goes seeking playful love.
Now the crane has stretched out
its neck, and is turning.

REFRAIN, for 5 voices, as before.

VERSE, for 3 voices.

The sun appears more beautiful,
more serene, clearer, rosier;
The thick cloud disappears
dissipated by the ray(s) of the great eye
    [= sun].
A thousand woods are full of greenery;
a thousand fields are full of greenery;
a thousand meadows [are full of]
    variegated flowers.

REFRAIN, for 5 voices, as before.

Le Soleil éclaire luizant
D'une plus séreine clairté:
Du nuage l'ombre s'enfuit,
Qui se jou' et court et noircit
Et foretz et champs et couteaus.
Le labeur humain reverdit,
Et la pré découvre ses fleurs.

REFRAIN: Revecy, etc.

70. APRIL IS IN MY MISTRESS' FACE, Madrigal
Thomas Morley (c. 1557-1602)

*To be pronounced *July* in conformity with the usage of Elizabethan days, as in *duly* and *truly*.

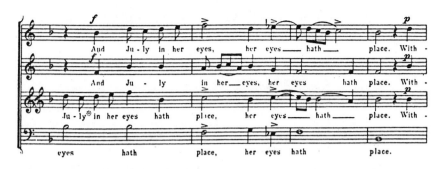

71. IN DARKNESS LET ME DWELL, Ayre
John Dowland (1563-1626)

72a. MEIN G'MÜTH IST MIR VERWIRRET, Lied
Hans Leo Hassler (1562–1612)

Mein gmüth ist mir verwirret
  Das macht ein Jungfrau zart
Bin gantz und gar verirret
  Mein herz das krenckt sich hart
Hab tag und nacht kein ruh
  Für allzeit grosse klag
Thu stets seufftzen und weinen
  In trauren schier verzag.

My peace of mind is disturbed
  This a tender maiden has caused
I am completely and entirely astray
  My heart hurts badly
Day and night I have no rest
  Always [there is] great complaint
Continual sighing and weeping
  In utter sorrow despairing.

Ach dass sie mich thet fragen
  Was doch dir ursach sey
Warumb ich führ solch klagen
  Ich wolt irs sagen frey
Dass sie allein die ist
  Die mich so sehr verwundt
Köndt ich ir Hertz erweichen
  Würd ich bald wider gesund.

Reichlich ist sie gezieret
  Mit schön thugend ohn ziel
Höflich wie sie gebüret
  Ihrs gleichen ist nich viel
Für andern Jungkfraun zart
  Führt sie allzeit den preiss
Wann ichs anschau, vermeine
  Ich sey im Paradeiss.

Ich kan nicht gnug erzehlen
  Ihr schön und thugend vil
Für alln wolt ichs erwehlen
  Wer es nur auch ir will
Dass sie ir Hertz und Lieb
  Gegn mir wendet allzeit
So würd mein schmertz und klagen
  Verkehrt in grosse freud.

Aber ich muss auffgeben
  Und allzeit traurig sein
Solts mir gleich kosten sLeben
  Das ist mein gröste pein
Dann ich bin ir zu schlecht
  Darumb sie mein nicht acht

Gott wolts für leid bewahren
  Durch sein Göttliche macht.

Ah, if she were to ask me
  What the matter is
Why I am complaining so
  I would say to her freely
That she alone is the one
  Who has wounded me so greatly
If I could soften her heart
  I would soon be healthy again.

She is richly adorned
  With beautiful virtue without end
As nobly as she is born
  Not many are equal to her
Against other tender maidens
  She always wins the prize
When I look at her, I think
  I am in Paradise.

I cannot extol enough
  Her beautiful and virtuous power
For the only thing I would choose
  If it were her desire also
That she would turn her heart and love
  Toward me forever.
Then would my pain and complaining
  Change to great joy.

But I must give up
  And be sorrowful forever
Even if it should cost me my life.
  That is my greatest pain.
Because I am too low for her,
  That is why she does not consider
  me.
God will preserve me in [my] sorrow
  Through his Divine power.

72b. O HAUPT VOLL BLUT UND WUNDEN, Chorale
J. S. Bach (1685-1750)

O Haupt voll Blut und Wunden,
voll Schmerz und voller Hohn!
O Haupt, zu Spott gebunden
mit einer Dornenkron!
O Haupt, sonst schön gezieret
mit höchster Ehr' und Zier,
jetzt aber hoch schimpfieret:
Gegrüsset seist du mir!

Du edles Angesichte,
vor dem sonst schrickt und scheut
das grosse Weltgerichte,
wie bist du so bespeit!
Wie bist du so erbleichet,
wer hat dein Augenlicht,
dem sonst kein Licht nicht gleichet,
so schändlich zugericht'?

O head full of blood and wounds,
full of sorrow and full of scoffing!
O head, for mockery, wreathed
with a crown of thorns!
O head, once handsomely adorned
with highest honor and esteem,
but now highly insulted:
Let me hail You!

You, noble countenance,
before which the great Last Judgment
terrifies and cowers,
how You are spat upon!
How very pale you are!
Who has so shamefully treated
Your eyes' light [literally, eyesight]
which no other light equals?

73. TODOS LOS BIENES DEL MUNDO, Villancico
Juan del Encina (1468–c. 1530)

Source: Universita degli Studi di Firenze Instituto Ispanico, 1974. Casa Editrice D'Anna.

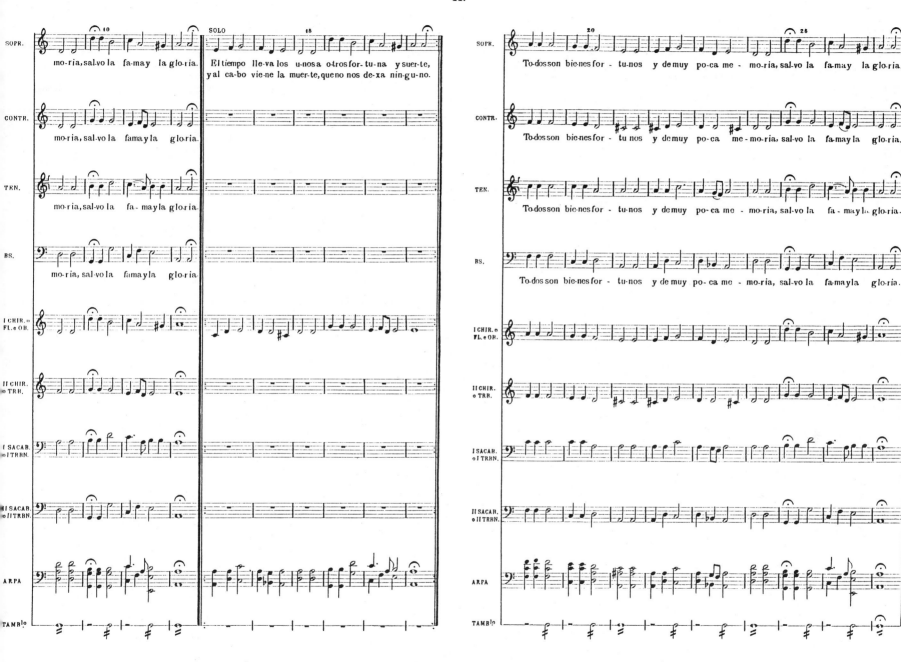

118

Todos los bienes del mundo
passan presto y su memoria,
salvo la fama y la gloria.

El tiempo lleva los unos
a otros fortuna y suerte,

y al cabo viene la muerte,
que no nos dexa ninguno.

Todos son bienes fortunos
y de muy poca memoria,
salvo la fama y la gloria.

La fama vive segura,
aunque se muera su dueño;
los otros bienes son sueño
y una cierta sepultura.

La mejor y más ventura
passa presto y su memoria,
salvo la fama y la gloria.

Procuremos bona fama,
que jamás nunca se pierde,
árbol que siempre está verde
y con el fruto en la rama.

Todo bien que bien se llama
passa presto y su memoria,
salvo la fama y la gloria.

—Juan del Encina

All the goods [or, property] in the world
and their memory pass quickly,
except fame [or, reputation] and glory.

Time carries away some,
others [are taken away] by fortune and
    luck,
and in the end death comes,
which leaves us with none.

All goods are from fortune
and [are] of very short memory,
except fame [= reputation] and glory.

Fame [reputation] survives safely
even if its owner dies;
the other goods are a dream
and [have] a certain grave.

The best and greatest venture
and its memory pass quickly,
except fame [reputation] and glory.

Let us acquire good reputation,
which never, never is lost,
a tree that always is green
and with fruit on the [its] branches.

All property that can be called good
and its memory passes quickly,
except reputation [fame] and glory.

—Miguel Roig-Francoli

74. EGO SUM PANIS VIVUS, Motet
William Byrd (c. 1543–1623)

Reproduced by permission of Oxford University Press, Oxford, England.

Ego sum panis vivus,
qui de coelo descendi:
Si quis manducaverit
ex hoc pane,
vivet in aeternum.
Alleluia.

I am the living bread,
which came down from heaven:
If any man eats
of this bread,
he shall live for ever.
Alleluia.

—Biblia Sacra, Evangelium secundum
Joannem, 6:51–52.

—Holy Bible, St. John, 6:51

75. LAUDA SION, Motet
Giovanni Pierluigi da Palestrina (c. 1525-1594)

Reprinted by permission of Gregg Publishing Company, Ltd., White Swan House, Godstone, Surrey, England RH9 8LW.

Lauda Sion Salvatorem,
Lauda ducem et pastorem,
in hymnis et canticis;
Quantum potes, tantum aude:
Quia major omni laude,
nec laudare sufficis.

Bone pastor, panis vere,
Jesu, nostri miserere;
Tu nos pasce, nos tuere,
Tu nos bona fac videre
in terra viventium.

Amen.

Zion, praise [your] Saviour,
Praise [your] leader and shepherd,
in hymns and canticles;
as much as you are able, so much dare:
because [He is] greater than all praise,
nor can you praise [Him] enough.

Good shepherd, true bread,
Jesus, have mercy on us;
You feed us, protect us,
You make us see good things
in the land of the living.

Amen.

76. MISSA LAUDA SION, Kyrie
Giovanni Pierluigi da Palestrina (c. 1525–1594)

Kyrie eleison	Lord have mercy
Christe eleison	Christ have mercy
Kyrie eleison	Lord have mercy

77. O VOS OMNES, Motet
Tomás Luis de Victoria (1548–1611)

Cantus.

Altus.

Tenor.

Bassus.

Source: Breitkopf and Härtel, Wiesbaden, Germany.

O vos omnes,
qui transitis per viam,
attendite et videte
si est dolor
sicut dolor meus.

O, all you
who pass along the way,
behold and see
if there is any sorrow
like unto my sorrow.

—Biblia Sacra, Lamentationes, 1:12

—Holy Bible, Lamentations, 1:12

78. TRISTIS EST ANIMA MEA, Motet
Orlande de Lassus (1532-1594)

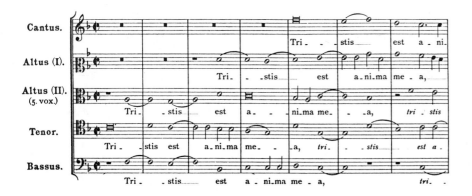

Source: Breitkopf and Härtel, Wiesbaden, Germany.

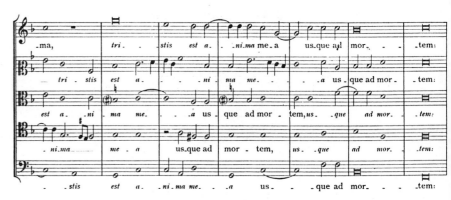

Tristis est anima mea, usque ad mortem;
sustinete hic, et vigilate mecum:
nunc videbitis turbam,
quae circumdabit me:
vos fugam capietis,
et ego vadam immolari pro vobis.

My soul is sorrowful, even unto death;
tarry ye here, and watch with me:
now you will see the crowd,
that will surround me:
you will take flight,
and I shall go to be sacrificed for you.

(from The Bible, Matt. 26:38, Mark 14:34, and Liber Usualis, 630)

79. SONATA PIAN' E FORTE
Giovanni Gabrieli (c. 1553–1612)

128

80. Excerpt from GAUDE DEI GENITRIX,
Versets on the Sequence
Arnolt Schlick (c. 1460-1522)

II. Discantus ex bassu in decimis
Vagans ex tenore in quartis

III. Discantus ex tenore in sextis
Vagans ex bassu in tertiis

81. RECERCAR QUARTO
Girolamo Cavazzoni (c. 1525–c. 1578)

*two eighth notes

82. LA STRADA, Canzona
Tarquinio Merula (c. 1594–1665)

Source: Breitkopf and Härtel, Wiesbaden, Germany.

83. IN NOMINE

a. Gloria tibi trinitas
Anonymous Sarum Chant

Glo - ri - a ti - bi - tri - ni - tas ae - qua - lis, u - na De - i - tas

et an - te om - ni - a sae - cu - la,

et nunc, et in per - pe - tu - um

b. In nomine
John Bull (c. 1562–1628)

From J. A. Fuller Maitland and W. Barclay Squire, *The Fitzwilliam Virginal Book*. Reprinted by permission of Dover Publications, Inc., Mineola, NY.

*G sharp in the MS.
**Crotchet in MS.
***Crotchet and 2 quavers in MS.

84. DIFERENCIAS SOBRE EL CANTO LLANO DEL CABALLERO
Antonio de Cabezón (1510–1566)

Institut für Mittelalterliche Musikforschung.

85. EL MAESTRO: FANTASIA NO. 17
Luys de Milán (c. 1500-c. 1561)

Transcribed from Tablature by Robert Ferguson. Used by permission.

86. IL TRANSILVANO: TOCCATA NO. 13
Girolamo Diruta (c. 1554-c. 1611)

[fol. 34]

[fol. 34ᵛ]

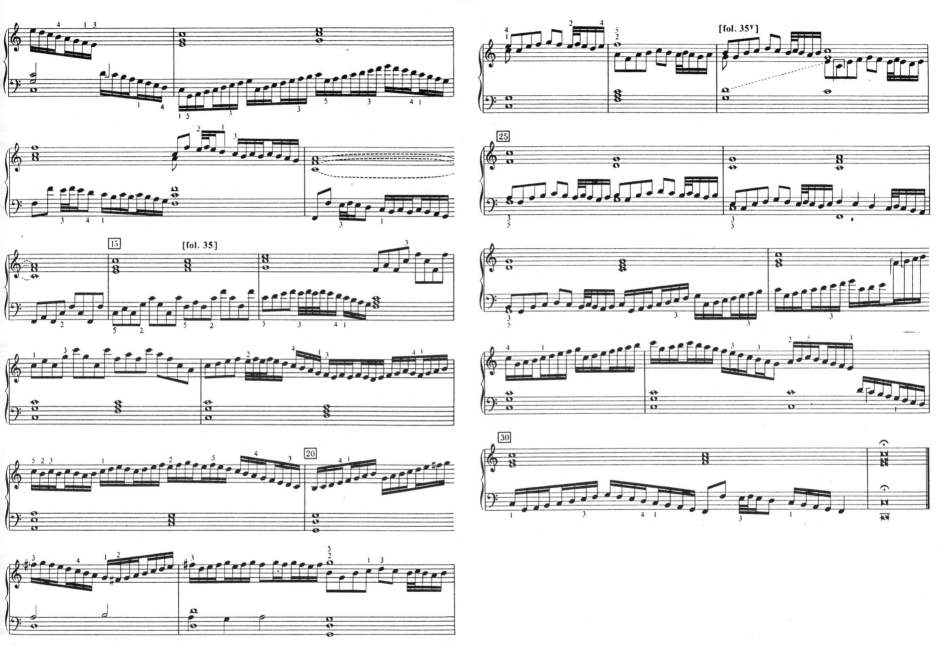

87. IN ECCLESIIS
Giovanni Gabríeli (c. 1553–1612)

From *Opera Omnia,* 1969 by American Institute of Musicology/Hänssler-Verlag, D-73762
Neuhausen-Stuttgart, Germany. Reprinted by permission.

In ecclesiis benedicite Domino.
Alleluia.

In omni loco dominationis,
    benedic anima mea Dominum.
Alleluia.

In Deo salutari meo, et gloria mea.
Deus auxilium meum et spes mea in
    Deo est.
Alleluia.

Deus noster, te invocamus,
    te laudamus, te adoramus.
Libera nos, salva nos, vivifica nos.
Alleluia.

Deus, adiutor noster in aeternum.
Alleluia.

In the congregations, bless the Lord.
Alleluia.

In every place in the dominion,
    bless the Lord, [O] my soul.
Alleluia.

In God [is] my salvation, and my glory.
God [is] my help and my hope is in
    God.
Alleluia.

Our God, we invoke Thee,
    we praise Thee, we worship Thee.
Deliver us, save us, give us life.
Alleluia.

God, our helper in eternity.
Alleluia.

88. AMARILLI MIA BELLA, Madrigal
Giulio Caccini (c. 1545-1618)

*The realization is after Robert Dowland's (1610).

This music is reproduced by permission of A-R Editions, Inc. It is taken from Giulio Caccini: *Le nuove musiche,* edited by H. Wiley Hitchcock, published as volume 9 of *Recent Researches in the Music of the Baroque Era,* by A-R Editions, Inc., 801 Deming Way, Madison, WI 53717. Copyright 1970 A-R Editions, Inc.

89. DAFNE, "Bella ninfa fuggitiva," Chorus
Jacopo Corsi (1561–1602)

Brus, fols. 53-54
(No. 34)

Amarilli, mia bella,	Amarillis, my beautiful one,
Non credi, o del mio cor dolce desio,	Do you not believe, oh, my heart's sweet desire,
D'esser tu l'amor mio?	that you are my love?
Credilo pur, e se timor t'assale,	Believe it, by all means! and if fear assails you,
Prendi questo mio strale,	Take this, my arrow,
A primi il petto,	Open [my] breast,
e vedrai scritto in core,	and you will see written on [my] heart,
Amarilli è 'l mio amore.	"Amarillis is my love."

Bella ninfa fuggitiva
  sciolt' e priva
  Del mortal tuo nobil velo,
  Godi pur pianta novella,
  Casta e bella,
  Car' al mondo, e car' al cielo.

Beautiful fugitive nymph,
  free and deprived
  of your noble mortal veil (= form),
  enjoy, too, the sad tale,
  [you who are] chaste and beautiful,
  dear to the world, and dear to the heavens.

From William V. Porter, "Peri and Corsi's Dafne: Some New Discoveries and Observations" in *Journal of the American Musicological Society,* Vol. XVIII, No. 2, Summer 1965. Copyright © 1965 American Musicological Society, Philadelphia, PA. Reprinted by permission of the author.

Tu non curi e nembi e tuoni:

Tu coroni
Cigni, regi, e dèi celesti:
Geli il cielo o 'nfiammi e scaldi,

Di smeraldi
Lieta ogn' or t'adorni e vesti.

Godi pur de' doni egregi;
I tuoi pregi
Non t'invidio e non desio:

Io, se mai d'amor m'assale
Aureo strale
Non vo' guerra con un Dio.

Se a fuggir movo le piante
Vero amante,
Contra amor cruda e superba,
Venir possa il mio crin d'auro
Non pur lauro,
Ma qual è più miser' erba.

Sia vil canna, il mio crin biondo

Che l'immondo
Gregge ogn' or schianti e dirame;

Sia vil fien, ch'a i crudi denti

De gli armenti
Tragga ogn' or l'avida fame.

Ma s' a' preghi sospirosi
Amorosi,
Di pietà sfavillo et ardo,
S'io prometto a l'altrui pene
Dolce spene
Con un riso e con un guardo,

You do not heed either clouds or
thunder:
You crown
swans, kings, and heavenly gods:
whether the sky is frosty or inflamed
and warm,
with emeralds
you, rejoicing, clothe and adorn
yourself constantly.

Enjoy, too, the noble gifts;
your treasures
I do not envy you and I do not desire
[them];
I, if ever I am assailed by love's
golden arrow,
do not want to fight a god.

If I must die to flee the plaint
of a true lover,
against love cruel and proud,
may my golden hair not become
pure (i.e., chaste) laurel,
but that which is a much more lowly
plant.

May my blond hair be a cheap
[= lowly] reed
that the grimy
flock [or, herd] snaps off and prunes
every day;
may it be hay of little worth, that,
with cruel teeth,
the greedy appetites of the herds
pull up every day.

But if, with sighing, prayers,
loving,
with compassion, I glow and I burn,
If I promise for another's suffering
sweet hope
with a laugh and with a glance,

Non soffrir, cortese Amore,
Che 'l mio ardore
Prenda a scherno alma gelata;

Non soffrir ch' in piaggia o 'n lido

Cor infido
M'abbandoni innamorata.

Fa' ch' al foco de' miei lumi
Si consumi
Ogni gelo, ogni durezza;
Ardi poi quest' alma allora
Ch' altra adora,
Qual si sia la mia bellezza.

—Ottavio Rinuccini

Do not grieve, kind Love,
because my ardor
holds in scorn [= is not repelled by]
a cold spirit;
do not grieve because on the slopes or
on the shore
unfaithful heart
[my] beloved abandons me.

By the fire of my eyes cause
to be dissipated
every chill, every difficulty;
then warm this sweet laurel tree
that adores another,
so that that beautiful one may be
mine.

90. CRUDA AMARILLI, Madrigal
Claudio Monteverdi (1567-1643)

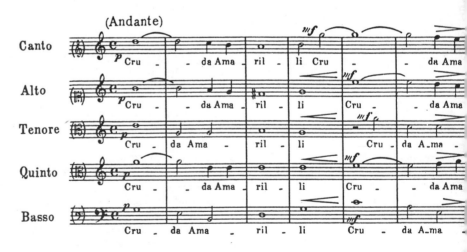

Monteverdi MADRIGAL: CRUDA AMARILLI, edited by Malipiero. Used by kind permission of European American Music Distributors Corporation, sole U.S. and Canadian agent for Universal Edition.

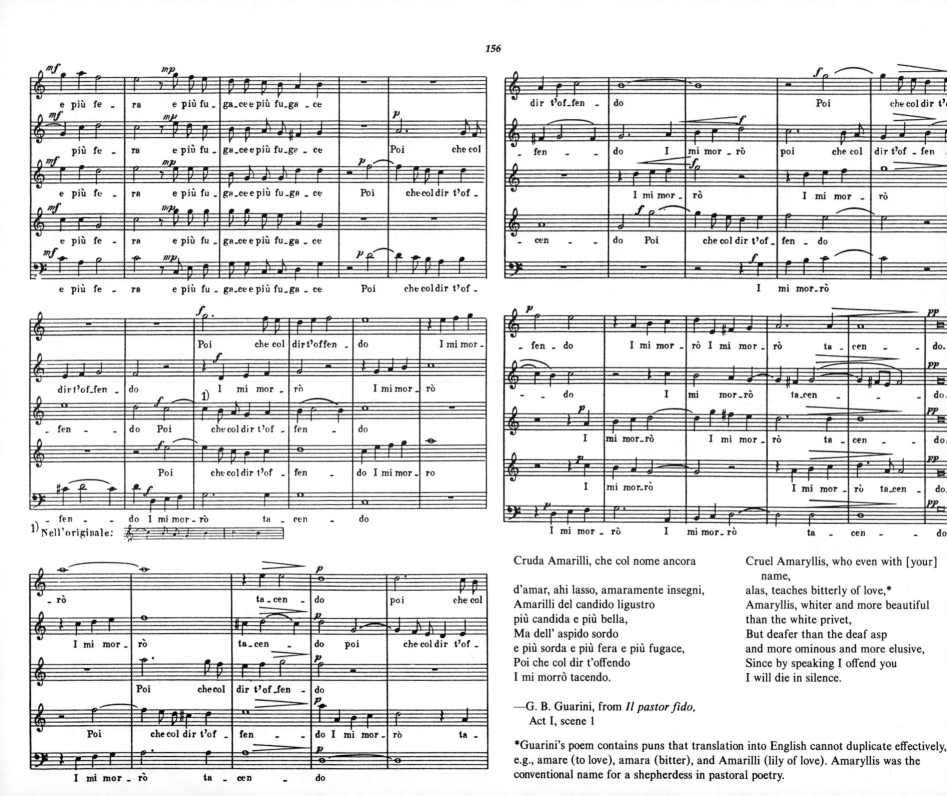

Cruda Amarilli, che col nome ancora

d'amar, ahi lasso, amaramente insegni,
Amarilli del candido ligustro
più candida e più bella,
Ma dell' aspido sordo
e più sorda e più fera e più fugace,
Poi che col dir t'offendo
I mi morrò tacendo.

—G. B. Guarini, from *Il pastor fido,*
   Act I, scene 1

Cruel Amaryllis, who even with [your] name,
alas, teaches bitterly of love,*
Amaryllis, whiter and more beautiful
than the white privet,
But deafer than the deaf asp
and more ominous and more elusive,
Since by speaking I offend you
I will die in silence.

*Guarini's poem contains puns that translation into English cannot duplicate effectively, e.g., amare (to love), amara (bitter), and Amarilli (lily of love). Amaryllis was the conventional name for a shepherdess in pastoral poetry.

91. L'ORFEO, Act III, "Possente spirto"
Claudio Monteverdi (1567-1643)

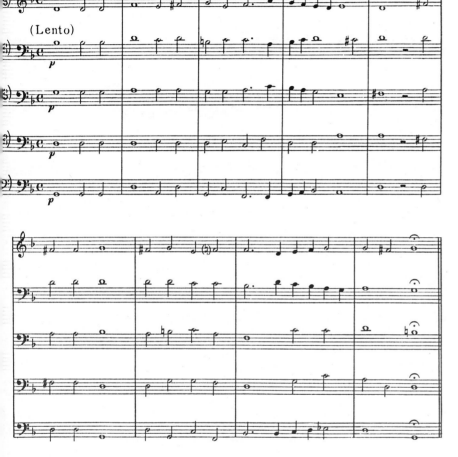

Monteverdi L'ORFEO, edited by Malipiero. Used by kind permission of European American Music Distributors Corporation, sole U.S. and Canadian agent for Universal Edition.

Orfeo al suono del organo di legno, e un chitarrone canta una sola de le due parti.

*(Accompanied by wood organ and a chitarrone, Orpheus sings only one of the two parts [preferably the ornamented one].)

Ritornello

DUOI CORNETTI

io che poi di vi _ _ ta è

che poi di vi _ ta è pri _

Non vi _ _ _ vo

Non vi _ _ v'io no

pri _ va mia ca _ ra spo _ sa

_ va mia ca _ ra spo _ sa

Ritornello

162

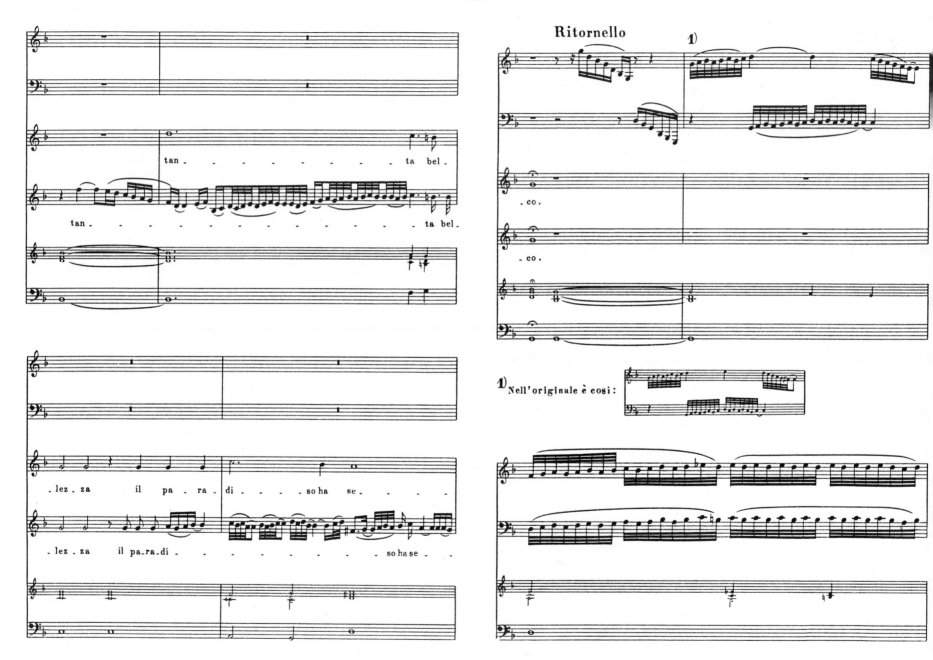

Ritornello

1)

1) Nell'originale è così:

164

1) A questo punto finisce la variazione: le due parti si riuniscono.
(Here the ornamented version ends; the two parts become one.)

ahi chi nie_ga il con_for_to a le mie pe_ne.

Furno sonate le altre parti da tre Viole da braccio, et un contrabasso de Viola tocchi pian piano.

(ORFEO)

Sol tu no_bi_le Dio puoi dar_mia_i_ta

Ne te_mer dei che sopr'un'au_rea ce_tra Sol di cor_de so_

_a_vi ar_mo le di_ _ta Con_tra cui ri_gi_

_d'al_ma in_van s'im_pe_ _tra.

CARONTE

Ben mi lu_sin_ga al_quan_to dilet_tan_domi il co_ re sconso_la_to canto_

166

ORFEO:
Possente spirto e formidabil nume,
senza cui far passaggio a l'altra riva

alma da corpo sciolta in van presume.

INSTRUMENTAL RITORNELLO

Non viv' io, no, che poi di vita è priva
mia cara sposa, il cor non è più meco,

e senza cor com' esser può ch'io viva?

INSTRUMENTAL RITORNELLO

A lei volto ho il cammin per l'aer cieco,

a l'inferno non già, ch'ovunque stassi
tanta bellezza il paradiso ha seco.

INSTRUMENTAL RITORNELLO

Orfeo son io, che d'Euridice i passi
segue per queste tenebrose arene,
ove giammai per uom mortal non vassi.
O de le luci mie luci serene,
s'un vostro sguardo può tornarmi in vita,

ahi, chi niega il conforto a le mie pene?
Sol tu, nobile dio, puoi darmi aita,
né temer dei, che sopra un'aurea cetra
sol di corde soavi armo le dita
contra cui rigida alma in van s'impetra.

CARONTE:
Ben mi lusinga alquanto
dilettandomi il core,
sconsolato cantore,
il tuo pianto e 'l tuo canto.
Ma lunge, ah, lunge sia da questo petto
pietà, di mio valor non degno effetto.

ORPHEUS:
Powerful spirit and formidable god,
without whom souls released from the body

presume in vain to cross to the other bank.

INSTRUMENTAL RITORNELLO

I am not alive, no, since my dear wife
was deprived of life, [my] heart is no longer with me,

and without a heart how is it possible for me to live?

INSTRUMENTAL RITORNELLO

To her have I turned [my] way through the dark air,

not already to Hades, but wherever
so much beauty is, paradise is with her.

INSTRUMENTAL RITORNELLO

I am Orfeo, who follows Euridice's steps
through these dark arenas
where mortal man never has access.
O, serene lights of my lights [= eyes],
if one of your glances is able to restore life,

oh, who denies solace to my distress?
You alone, noble god, can give [me] aid,
do not fear the gods, since [my] fingers
over the sweet strings of a golden lyre
are [my] only weapon against the stern souls to whom entreaty is in vain.

CHARON:
I am much flattered by such
delight to my heart,
disconsolate singer,
by your lament and by your song.
But far, ah, far from my breast
is pity, which is beneath my dignity.

ORFEO:
Ahi, sventurato amante!
Sperar dunque non lice
ch' odan miei prieghi i cittadin d'Averno?
Onde, qual ombra errante
d'insepolto cadavere e infelice
privo sarò del cielo e de l'inferno?

Così vuol empia sorte
che in quest' orror di morte
da te, cor mio, lontano
chiami tuo nome in vano
e pregando e piangendo io mi consumi?

Rendetemi il mio ben, tartarei numi!

—A. Striggio

ORPHEUS:
Alas, unhappy lover [that I am]!
That I am not allowed to hope
that the citizens of Hades will not listen to my pleas?
Must I, therefore, like an errant shadow
of an unburied and unhappy corpse,
be deprived of heaven and of hell?

Does impious fate will it thus
that I, in this horror of death
far from you, my beloved,
call your name in vain
and consume myself in imploring and weeping?
Give me back my love, gods of Hell!

92. LA GRISELDA, Act II, Scene 4
Alessandro Scarlatti (1660-1725)

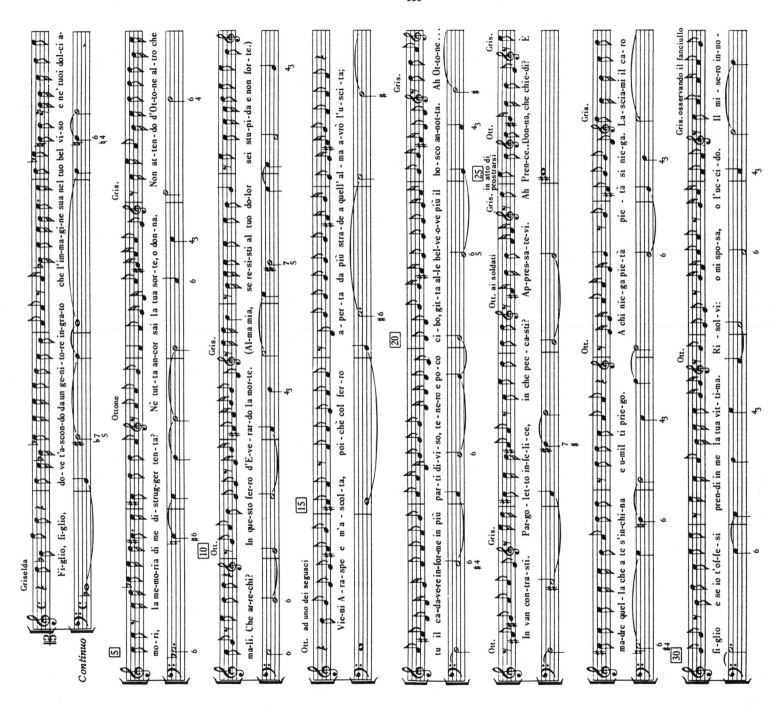

From the publishers of *The Operas of Alessandro Scarlatti Volume 3, Griselda*, edited by Donald J. Grout, Cambridge, Massachusetts. Harvard University Press, Copyright © 1975 by the President and Fellows of Harvard College. Reprinted by permission.

Aria

Andante moderato

RECITATIVE

QUEEN GRISELDA:

Figlio, figlio, dove t'ascondo da un
genitore ingrato che l'immagine sua
nel tuo bel viso e ne' tuoi dolci amori,
la memoria di me distrugger tenta?

OTTONE:

Nè tutta ancor sai la tua sorte, o donna.

GRISELDA:

Non attendo d'Ottone altro che mali.
Che arrechi?

OTTONE:

In questo ferro d'Everardo la morte.

GRISELDA:

(Alma mia, se resisti al tuo dolor sei
stupide e non forte.)

OTTONE: (ad uno dei seguaci)

Vieni Araspe e m'ascolta, poichè col
ferro aperta da più strade a quell'
alma avrò l'uscita; tu il cadavere
informe in più parti diviso, tenero e
poco cibo, gitta alle belve ove più il
bosco annotta.

GRISELDA:

Ah, Ottone . . .

OTTONE:

In van contrasti,

GRISELDA:

Son, son, where do I hide you from an
ungrateful father who is trying to
destroy his own likeness in your
handsome face, and in your sweet
love, the memory of me?

OTTONE:

You do not yet know all of your fate, O
woman.

GRISELDA:

I do not expect from Ottone anything
but evil. What do you bring?

OTTONE:

In this sword, death for Everardo.

GRISELDA:

(My soul, if you resist in your grief you
are stupid and not strong.)

OTTONE: (to one of his followers)

Come, Araspe, and listen to me. After
you have opened the way out for this
soul, by several paths, with the
sword, cut the shapeless corpse into
many pieces, [as] tender little bits of
food, and cast [them] to the wild
beasts where the woods is darkest.

GRISELDA:

Ah, Ottone . . .

OTTONE:

In vain you resist,

GRISELDA:

Pargoletto infelice, in che peccasti?

OTTONE: (ai soldati)

Appressatevi.

GRISELDA: (in atto di prostrarsi)

Ah Prence . . .

OTTONE:

Donna, che chiedi?

GRISELDA:

È madre quella che a te s'inchina e umil
ti priego.

OTTONE:

A chi niega pietà pietà si niega.

GRISELDA:

Lasciami il caro figlio e se io t'offesi
prendi in me la tua vittima.

OTTONE:

Risolvi: o mi sposa, o l'uccido.

GRISELDA: (osservando il fanciullo)

Il misero innocente tien fisse in me le
pupillette e nulla sa della sua
sciagura.

GRISELDA:

Unfortunate baby, in what have you
sinned?

OTTONE: (to the soldiers)

Draw near.

GRISELDA: (prostrating herself)

Ah, Prince . . .

OTTONE:

Woman, what do you ask?

GRISELDA:

The woman who bows before you and
humbly begs you is a mother.

OTTONE:

To the one who denies pity, pity is
denied.

GRISELDA:

Leave me my dear son, and if I have
offended you, take me as your victim.

OTTONE:

Decide: either marry me, or I will kill
him.

GRISELDA: (looking at the little boy)

The unfortunate innocent one keeps his
little eyes fixed on me and knows
nothing of his misfortune.

OTTONE:

Griselda, se più tardi non sei più madre, io già misuro il colpo che Gualtiero m'impose.

GRISELDA:

(Ingiusto padre!)

OTTONE:

E già eseguisco la crudel sentenza che tu stessa confermi.

GRISELDA:

Io?

OTTONE:

Sì, col tuo rifiuto.

GRISELDA:

Nè ti move il mio pianto?

OTTONE:

Lo bevano le arene.

GRISELDA:

Nè ti rendi a' miei prieghi?

OTTONE:

Li disperdano i venti.

GRISELDA:

Nè t'appaga il mio sangue?

OTTONE:

Griselda, if you delay longer, you will no longer be a mother; I am already measuring the blow that Gualtiero imposed on me.

GRISELDA:

(Unjust father!)

OTTONE:

And already I am carrying out the cruel sentence that you yourself confirm.

GRISELDA:

I?

OTTONE:

Yes, with your refusal.

GRISELDA:

Don't my tears move you?

OTTONE:

Let the soil drink them.

GRISELDA:

Nor do my prayers move you?

OTTONE:

Let the winds scatter them.

GRISELDA:

Nor does my blood appease you?

OTTONE:

Io voglio quello che scorre nelle vene al tuo Everardo.

GRISELDA:

Gualtier?

OTTONE:

Questa è sua legge.

GRISELDA:

Otton?

OTTONE:

. . . siane il ministro.

GRISELDA:

Il Ciel?

OTTONE:

. . . non ti difende.

GRISELDA:

Il Nume?

OTTONE:

È sordo.

GRISELDA:

E con darti la destra . . .

OTTONE:

Puoi madre salvar il figlio, sposa placar l'amante, e la man disarmar del ferro ignudo.

OTTONE:

I want that which flows in the veins of your Everardo.

GRISELDA:

Gualtiero?

OTTONE:

This is his order.

GRISELDA:

Ottone?

OTTONE:

. . . is to be his minister.

GRISELDA:

Heaven?

OTTONE:

. . . does not defend you.

GRISELDA:

God?

OTTONE:

. . . is deaf.

GRISELDA:

And by giving my hand . . .

OTTONE:

The mother can save her son, the bride can appease her lover, and can disarm the hand of the unsheathed sword.

GRISELDA:

Ubbidisci, ubbidisci, o crudel, svenalo,
    svenalo, o crudo!
(Gli lascia il fanciullo e parte
    risoluta. Poi nell' entrare si ferma
    alle voci d'Ottone, che stara in atto
    di ferire Everardo.)

OTTONE:

Madre di sasso: vedi, vedi con quanta
    rabbia nelle viscere tue la spada
    immergo, ecco che io già ferisco.

GRISELDA:

Ahi, che m'arresta il dolor, lo spavento,
    e fuggir semiviva indarno io tento
    dalla tragedia orribile e funesta.

ARIA

Figlio! Tiranno! O Dio!
Dite che far poss' io, che?
Dite che far poss' io, che?
O Dio! Figlio, figlio! Che far poss' io?
    Che far poss' io? Figlio!
Tiranno, tiranno, tiranno!   (Fine)
Che far poss' io? Tiranno, tiranno!
L'amor di madre amante mi squarcia,
    mi squarcia, mi squarcia in petto,
    mi squarcia in petto il cor, il cor,

ma il cor troppo costante
così squarciato ancor,
così squarciato ancor, vince, vince il suo
    affanno,
vince il suo affanno.
(Da capo al Fine)

GRISELDA:

Obey, obey, O cruel man, kill him, let
    him bleed to death, O cruel man!
(She leaves the child and resolutely
    starts to leave. As she is about to go,
    Ottone's voice stops her; he is in the
    act of stabbing Everardo.)

OTTONE:

Mother of stone: see, see with how much
    rage I plunge the blade into your
    viscera; behold that already I am
    striking.

GRISELDA:

Alas, that the grief stops me, the fright,
    and in vain I try, half alive, to flee
    from the horrible and fatal tragedy.

ARIA

Son! Tyrant! O God!
Tell me, what can I do, what?
Tell me, what can I do, what?
O God! Son, son! What can I do?
    What can I do? Son!
Tyrant, tyrant, tyrant!   (Fine)
What can I do? Tyrant, tyrant!
The love of a loving mother rends me,
    tears me, stabs me in the breast,
    tears my heart in my breast, my
    heart,
but the steadfast heart
even so torn apart,
even so torn apart, conquers, overcomes
    its suffering,
overcomes its suffering.
(Da capo al Fine)

93. ALCESTE, Ouverture
Jean-Baptiste Lully (1632-1687)

94. DIDO AND AENEAS, Act III, Dido: Recitative — Aria,
"Thy hand, Belinda" — "When I am laid in earth"
Henry Purcell (1659-1695)

*Aria ends here. Ritornello leads directly into Final Chorus: "With drooping wings."

95. JEPHTE, Conclusion, Oratorio
Giacomo Carissimi (1605–1674)

1. The manuscript copy made by M. A. Charpentier, Carissimi's pupil, concludes with measure 418; however, Chrysander's edition presents this expanded conclusion, derived from a manuscript now lost.

96. SYMPHONIAE SACRAE, Motet 9
O quam tu pulchra es, amica mea
Heinrich Schütz (1585–1672)

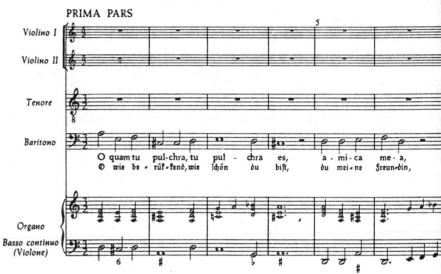

191

O quam tu pulchra es, amica mea, columba mea, formosa mea, immaculata mea!

O, how beautiful you are, my friend, my dove, my beauty, my undefiled one!

Oculi tui, oculi columbarum.

Your eyes, the eyes of a dove.

O quam tu pulchra es!

O, how beautiful you are!

Capilli tui, sicut greges caprarum.

Your hair is like a flock of she-goats.

O quam tu pulchra es!

O, how beautiful you are!

Dentos tui sicut greges tonsarum.

Your teeth are like a flock of [ewes] newly-shorn.

O quam tu pulchra es!

O, how beautiful you are!

Sicut vitta coccinea labia tua.

Your lips are as scarlet as the ribbon headband worn by sacrificial victims.

O quam tu pulchra es!

O, how beautiful you are!

Sicut turris David collum, collum tuum.

Your neck is like the tower of David.

O quam tu pulchra es!

O, how beautiful you are!

Duo ubera tua sicut duo hinnuli,

Your two breasts are like two young fawns,

sicut duo hinnuli capreae gemelli.

like two twin fawns that are roe deer.

O quam tu pulchra es!

O, how beautiful you are!

97. DIE SIEBEN WORTE . . . JESU CHRISTI AM KREUZ, Introit
Heinrich Schütz (1585-1672)

Da Jesus an dem Kreuze stund,
und ihm sein Leichnam war verwundt,
so gar mit bitterm Schmerzen,
die sieben Wort, die Jesus sprach,
betracht in deinem Herzen.

When Jesus was on the cross,
and his body was hurting him,
indeed, with bitter pain,
the seven words that Jesus spoke,
consider in your heart.

98. FANTASIA CHROMATICA
Jan Pieterzoon Sweelinck (1562-1621)

99. CANZONA PER L'EPISTOLA
Anonymous

100. SUITE XXII, in E minor
Johann Froberger (1616-1667)

Allemande.

Courante.

Sarabande.

Akademische Druck-u. Verlagsanstalt, Suite XXII, in E Minor by Johann Froberger (1616–1667).
Reprinted by permission.

Gigue.

101. IL SECONDO LIBRO DI TOCCATE: TOCCATA NONA
Girolamo Frescobaldi (1583–1643)

Non senza fatiga si giunge al fine

102. VATER UNSER IM HIMMELREICH, Chorale Preludes

a. Samuel Scheidt (1587–1654)

b. Dietrich Buxtehude (c. 1637–1707)

c. Johann Sebastian Bach (1685-1750)

103. MESSA DELLA MADONNA, RICERCAR DOPO IL CREDO
Girolamo Frescobaldi (1583-1643)

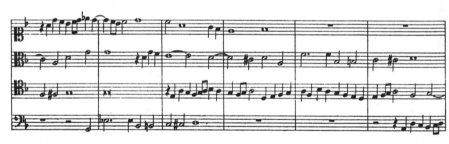

(ped. ped.)

104. PIÈCES DE CLAVECIN: SUITE IN D MINOR
Elisabeth-Claude Jacquet de la Guerre (c. 1666-1729)

La Flamande

From Elizabeth Jacquet de la Guerre: *Pièces de clavecin* Ed. Paul Brunold, Editions de l'Oiseau Lyre Monaco 1965.

Double

2e fois

[segue]

(*) dans l'original

209

Courante

Double

Sarabande

[*f* 2.ᵉ *fois*]

Gigue

Double

2me Gigue

105. VINGT-CINQUIÈME ORDRE
François Couperin (1668–1733)

a. La Visionaire

✱ *Ré . Fa* dans l'original

b. La Misterieuse

c. La Monflambert

Tendrement, sans lenteur

REPRISE

d. La Muse Victorieuse

e. **Les Ombres Errantes**

219

106. SONATA DA CAMERA, Op. 2, No. 4
Arcangelo Corelli (1653–1713)

Preludio

From © Laaber-Verlag, Germany.

Allemanda

Giga

107. SONATA DA CHIESA, Op. 5, No. 1
Arcangelo Corelli (1653–1713)

Corelli's Graces.

Grave.

Violino solo.

Violone e Cimbalo.

Allegro.

Tasto solo.

Reproduced by permission of Stainer & Bell Ltd., London, England.

108. CONCERTO IN A MAJOR, for Violin and Orchestra, Op. 9, No. 2, mvts. 1, 2
Antonio Vivaldi (1678–1741)

Boosey & Hawkes, Inc., New York, NY.

★) Edizione Le Cene:

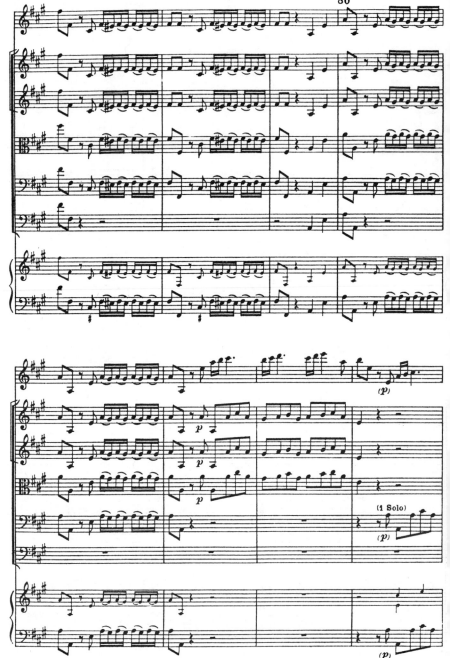

109. CASTOR ET POLLUX,
Act IV, Scene 1, "Séjour de l'éternelle paix"
Jean-Philippe Rameau (1683–1764)

Le théâtre représente les Champs-Elysées; diverses troupes d'Ombres heureuses paraissent dans l'éloignement.

238

Reproduced by arrangement with Broude Brothers Limited.

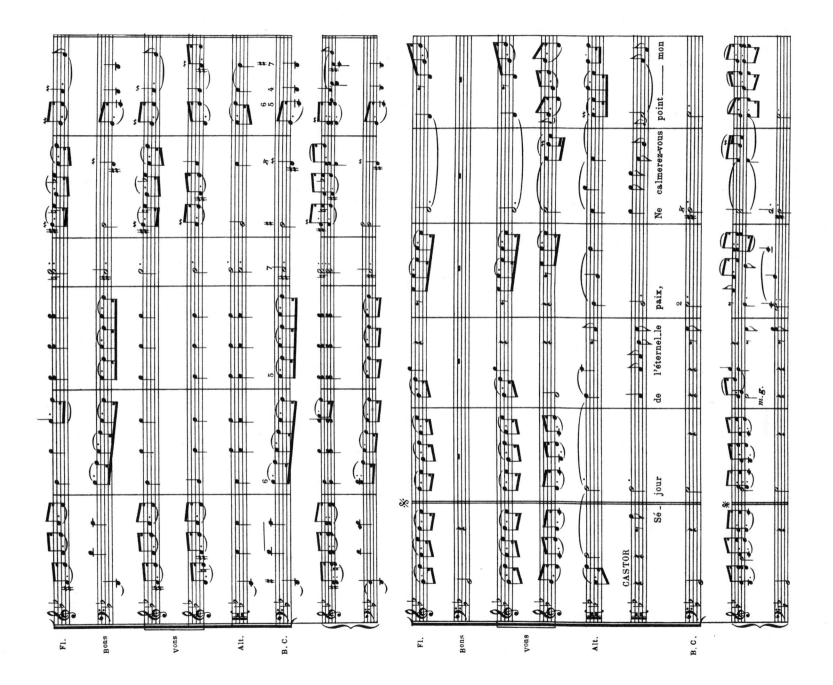

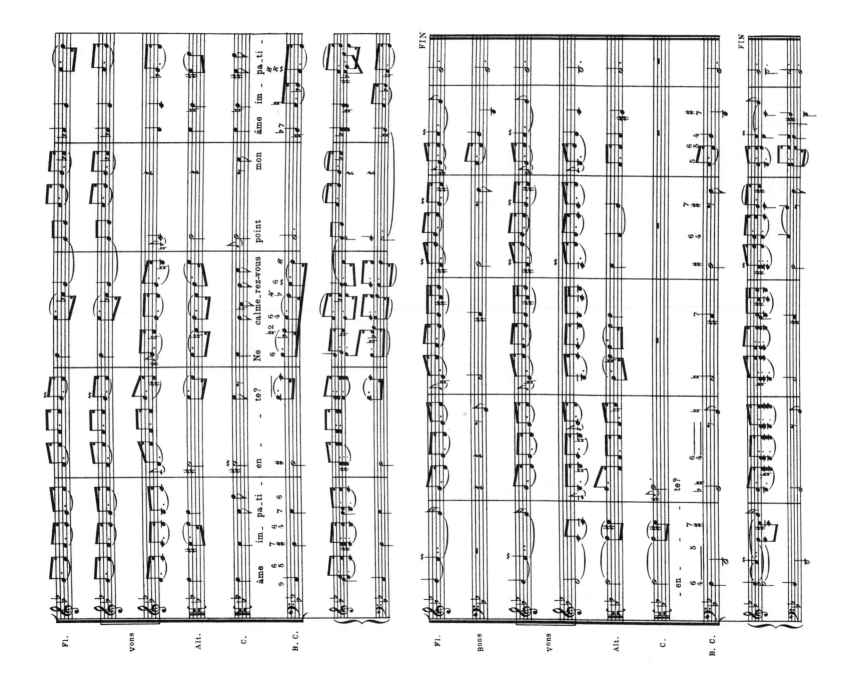

240

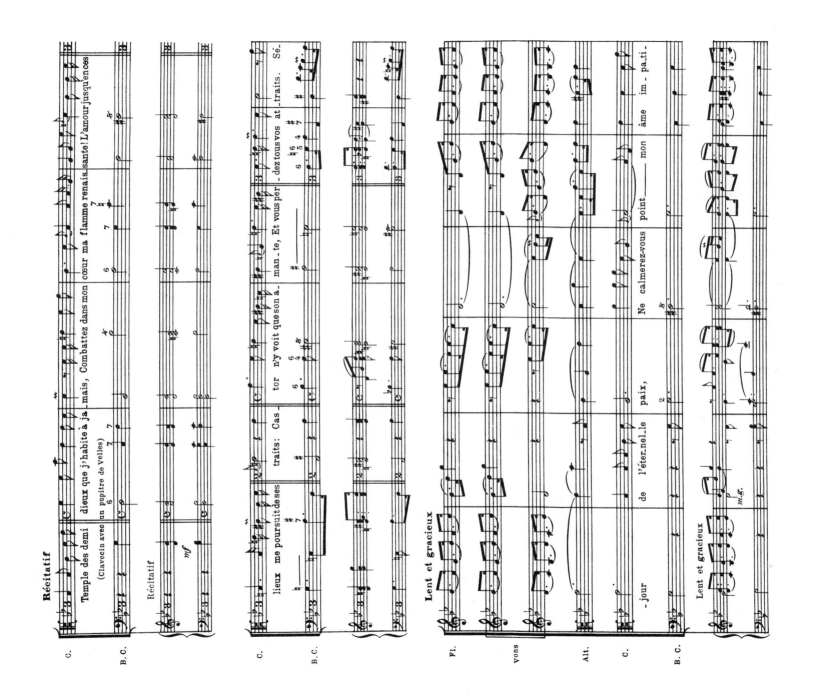

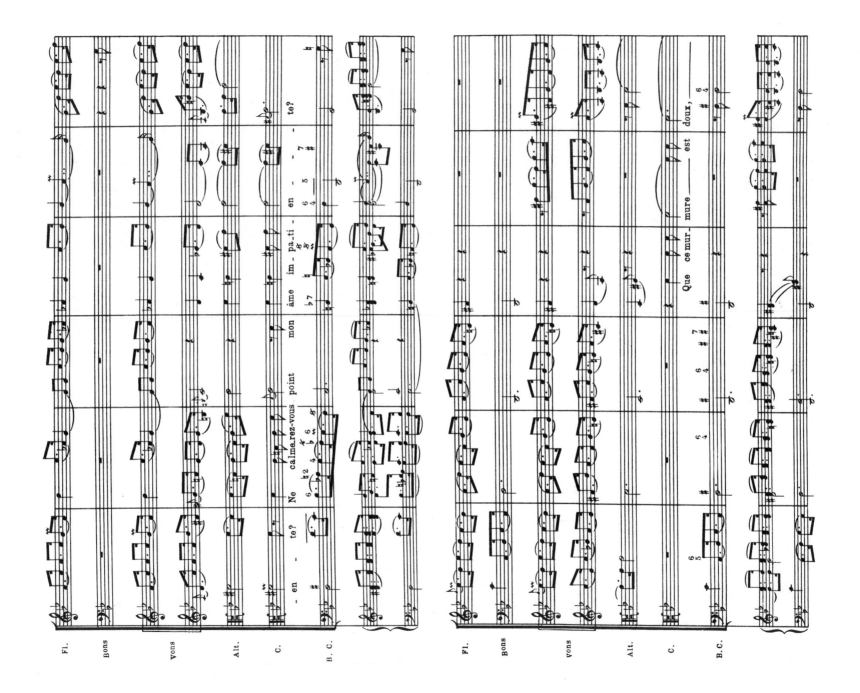

Séjour de l'éternelle paix,
Ne calmerez-vous point mon âme
impatiente?
Ne calmerez-vous point mon âme
impatiente?

Recitatif:

Temple des demi dieux que j'habite à
jamais,
Combattez dans mon coeur ma flamme
renaissante!
L'amour jusqu'en ces lieux me poursuit
de ses traits.
Castor n'y voit que son amante,
Et vous perdez tous vos attraits.

Aria:
Séjour de l'éternelle paix,
Ne calmerez-vous point mon âme
impatiente?
Ne calmerez-vous point mon âme
impatiente?

Que ce murmure est doux,
Que cet ombrage est frais!
De ces accords touchants la volupte
m'enchante!
Tout rit, tout prévient mon attente,

Et je forme encor des regrets!
Séjour de l'éternelle paix,
Ne calmerez-vous point mon âme
impatiente?
Ne calmerez-vous point mon âme
impatiente?

—from libretto by P.-J. Bernard

Abode of eternal peace,
Will you not calm my impatient soul at
all?
Will you not calm my impatient spirit at
all?

Recitative:

Temple of the demi-gods that I inhabit
forever,
Combat in my heart my reborn passion!

Love, even to these places, pursues me
with his darts.
Castor sees only his beloved there,
And you lose all your attractions.

Aria:
Abode of eternal peace,
Will you not calm my impatient soul at
all?
Will you not calm my impatient spirit at
all?

How sweet this murmur is!
How cool this shade is!
The voluptuousness of these touching
harmonies enchants me!
All is favorable, everything forestalls my
yearning,
And still I have some regrets!
Abode of eternal peace,
Will you not calm my impatient soul at
all?
Will you not calm my impatient spirit at
all?

110. L'ENHARMONIQUE, Clavecin Piece
Jean-Philippe Rameau (1683–1764)

111. JESU, MEINE FREUDE, Motet, mvt. 2
Johann Sebastian Bach (1685-1750)

Reprinted by permission of Hänssler Music Verlag GmbH.

112. ST. MATTHEW PASSION, Excerpts
Johann Sebastian Bach (1685–1750)

**a. Nos. 69–70. "Ach, Golgatha!" Recitative;
"Sehet, Jesus hat die Hand," Aria with Chorus**

252

RECITATIVE:

Ach, Golgatha, unsel'ges Golgatha!	Ah, Golgotha, accursed Golgotha!

Der Herr der Herrlichkeit muss
   schimpflich hier verderben,
	Here the Lord of heaven must be
	   disgracefully killed,

der Segen und das Heil der Welt wird
   als ein Fluch an's Kreuz gestellt.
	the blessed Saviour of the world will be
	   hanged on the cross like a malefactor.

Der Schöpfer Himmels und der Erden
   soll Erd' und Luft entzogen werden;
	The Creator of heaven and earth shall
	   be deprived of earth and sky;
	   [or, shall perish]

die Unschuld muss hier schuldig sterben.	the innocent must die here, as guilty.
Das gehet meiner Seele nah;	That grieves my soul;
Ach, Golgatha, unsel'ges Golgatha!	Ah, Golgotha, accursed Golgotha!

ARIA with CHORUS:

Soloist:	

Sehet, sehet, Jesus hat die Hand, uns zu
   fassen ausgespannt,
	See, see, Jesus has his hands
	   outstretched to grasp us,

kommt, kommt, in Jesu Armen sucht
   Erlösung.
	come, come, seek redemption in Jesus's
	   arms.

Chorus: Wohin?	Where?
Soloist:	

Lebet, lebet, sterbet, ruhet hier,
   ihr verlass'nen Kuchlein ihr,
	Live, die, rest here,
	   you forsaken little flock, [literally,
	   little chickens]

bleibet in Jesu Armen.	stay in Jesus's arms.
Chorus: Wo?	Where?
Soloist: Bleibet in Jesu Armen.	Remain in Jesus's arms.

b. No. 73. "Und siehe da, der Vorhang," Recitative; "Wahrlich, dieser ist Gottes Sohn gewesen," Chorus

Bach SAINT MATTHEW PASSION. © 1968 Ernst Eulenburg & Co GmbH, Mainz. All Rights Reserved. Used by permission of European American Music Distributors Corporation, sole U.S. and Canadian agent for Schott and Co., Ltd., London.

Recitative:

Und siehe da, der Vorhang im Tempel zerriss in zwei Stück, von oben an bis unten aus.	And behold, the veil [curtain] in the temple was ripped into two pieces, from the top to the bottom.
Und die Erde erbebete, und die Felten zerissen, und die Gräber taten sich auf, und stunden auf viel Leiber der Heiligen, die da schliefen; und gingen aus den Gräbern nach seiner Auferstehung, und kamen in die heilige Stadt, und erschienen vielen.	And the earth quaked, and the rocks split, and the graves opened, and there arose many bodies of the saints, who slept there; and they came out of the graves after his resurrection, and came into the Holy City, and appeared to many.
Aber der Hauptmann, und die bei ihm waren, und bewahreten Jesum, da sie sahen das Erdbeben, und was da geschah, erschraken sie sehr, und sprachen:	Now, the centurion, and those who were with him, and watching Jesus, when they saw the earthquake, and what happened there, they feared greatly, and said:

Chorus:

Wahrlich, dieser ist Gottes Sohn gewesen.	Truly, this was the Son of God.

113. DAS WOHLTEMPERIRTE KLAVIER [Volume I]:
Prelude and Fugue in C Minor, BWV 847
Johann Sebastian Bach (1685-1750)

a. Prelude

259

b. Fugue

114. DURCH ADAMS FALL IST GANZ VERDERBT, BMV 637,
Chorale Prelude
Johann Sebastian Bach (1685-1750)

115. Excerpts from MESSIAH
George Frideric Handel (1685–1759)

a. "Comfort ye," Accompanied Recitative

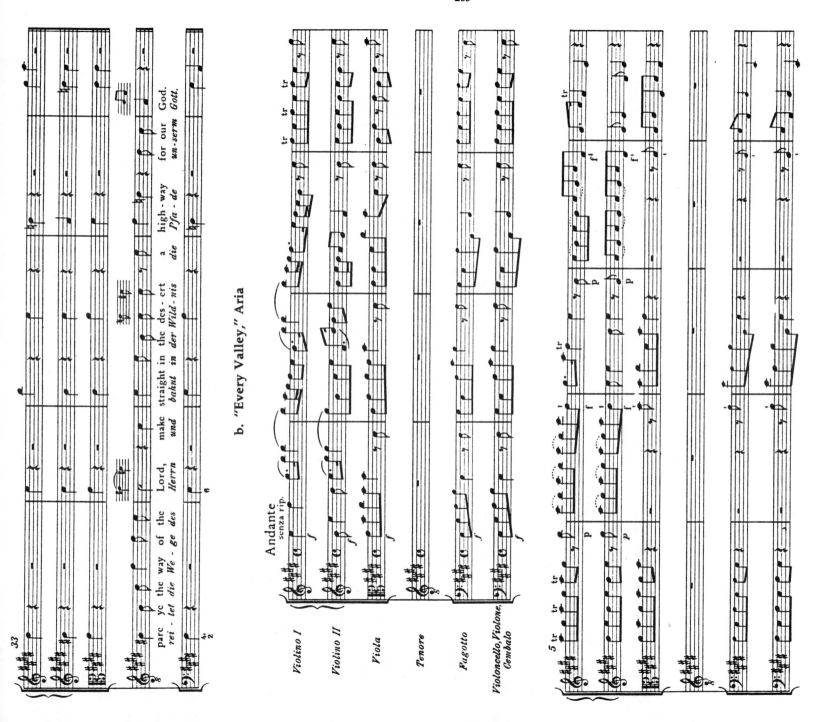

b. "Every Valley," Aria

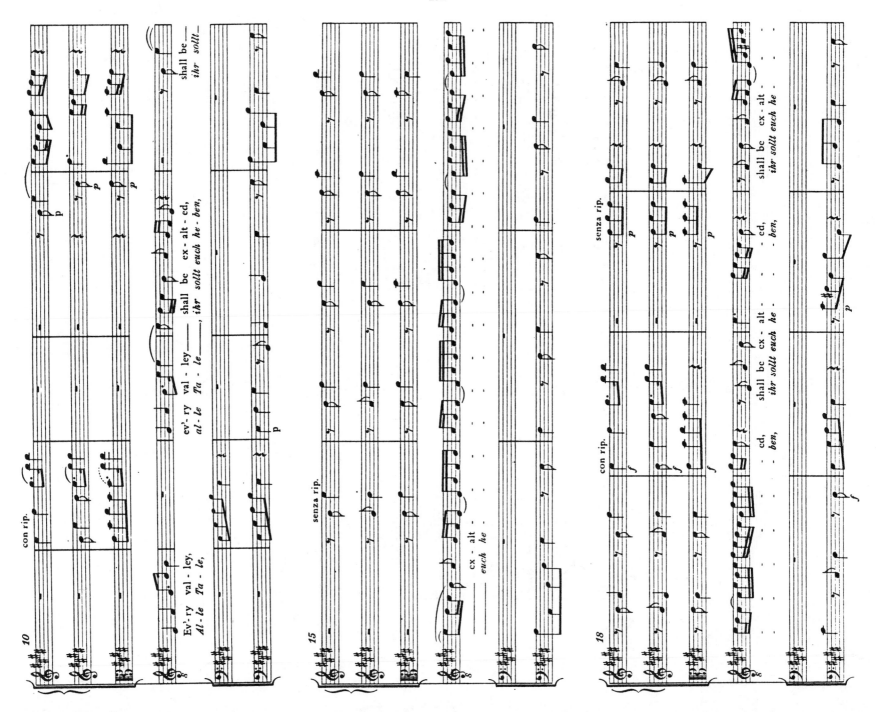

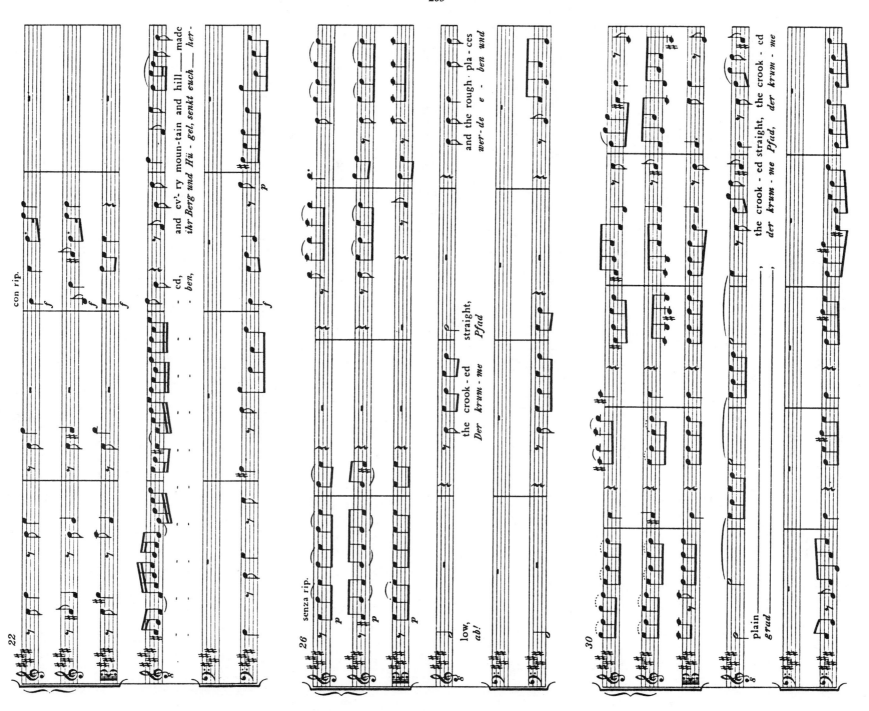

35

straight and the rough pla-ces plain.
Pfad wer-de e - ben und grad

tr
con rip.

Ev' - ry val - ley,
Al - le Ta - le,

40

—, and the rough pla-ces plain.
—, *wer-de e - ben und grad!*

senza rip.

46

ev' - ry val - ley —— shall be ex - alt -
al - le Ta - le ——, ihr sollt euch he -

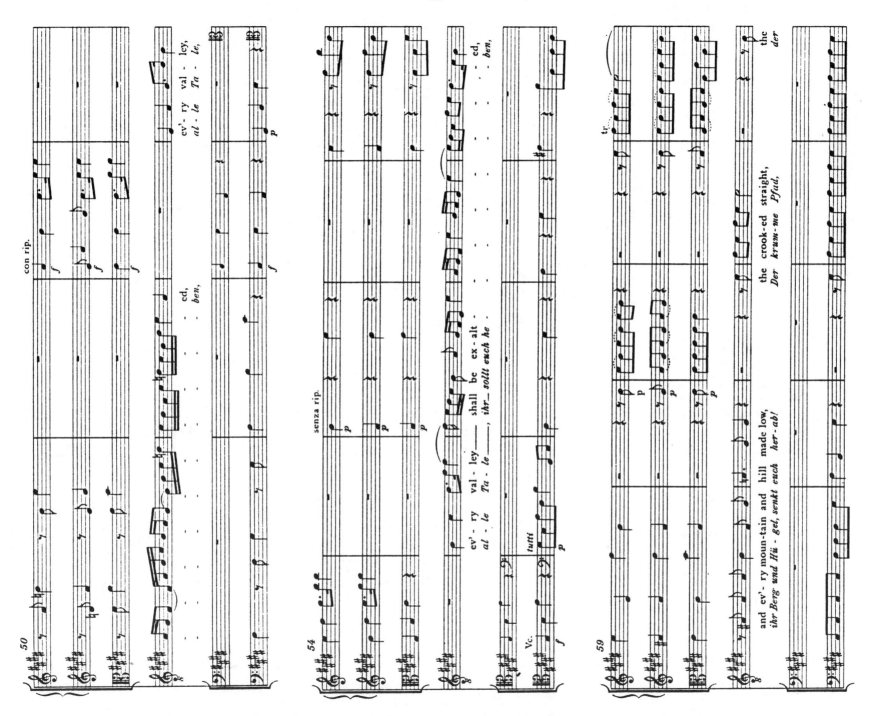

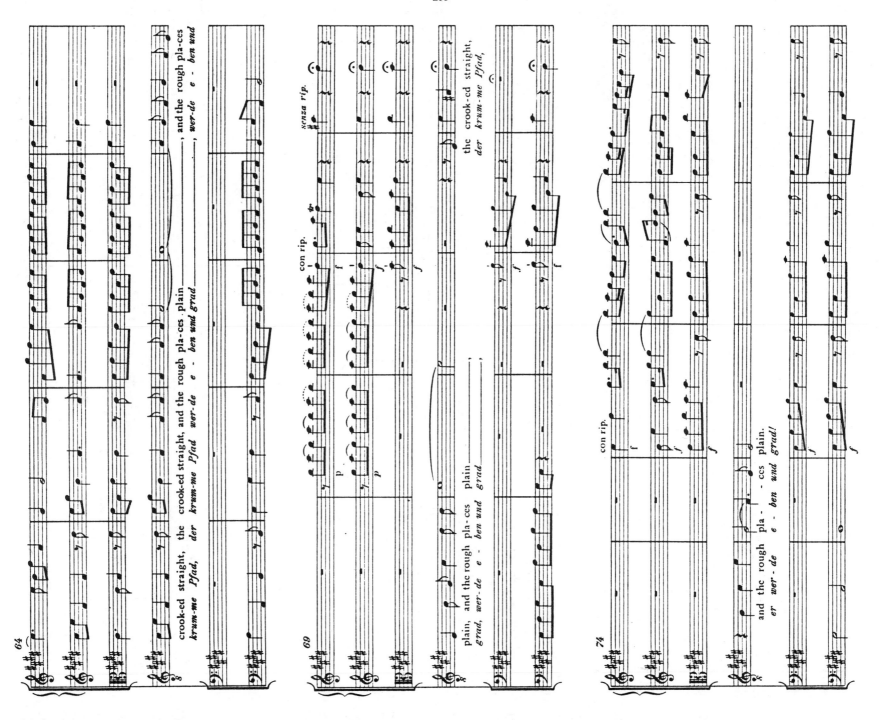

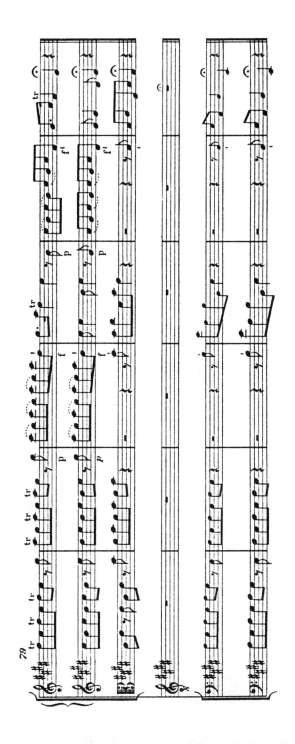

c. "All we like sheep," Chorus

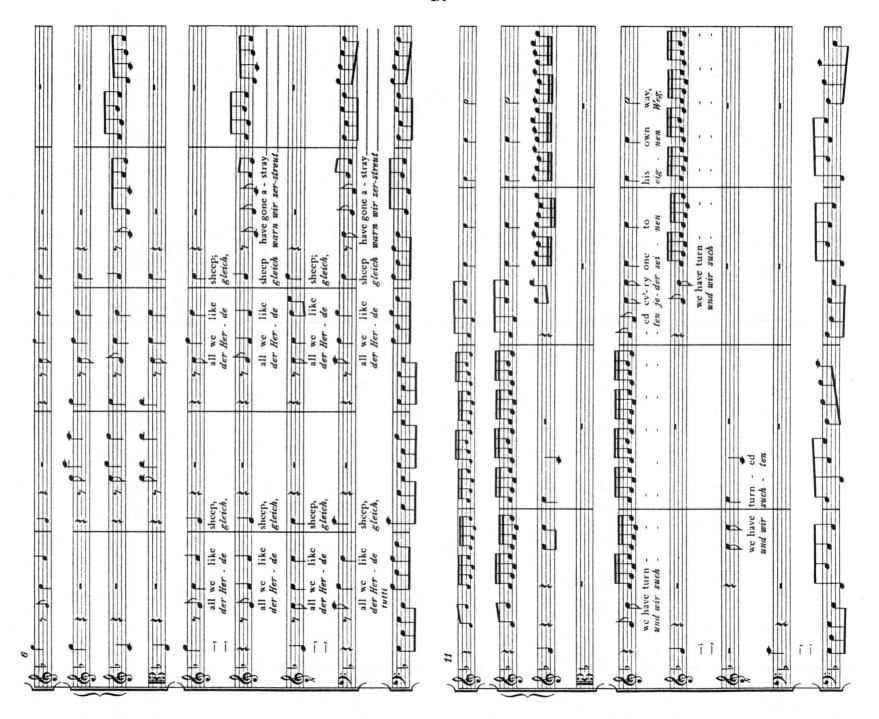

270

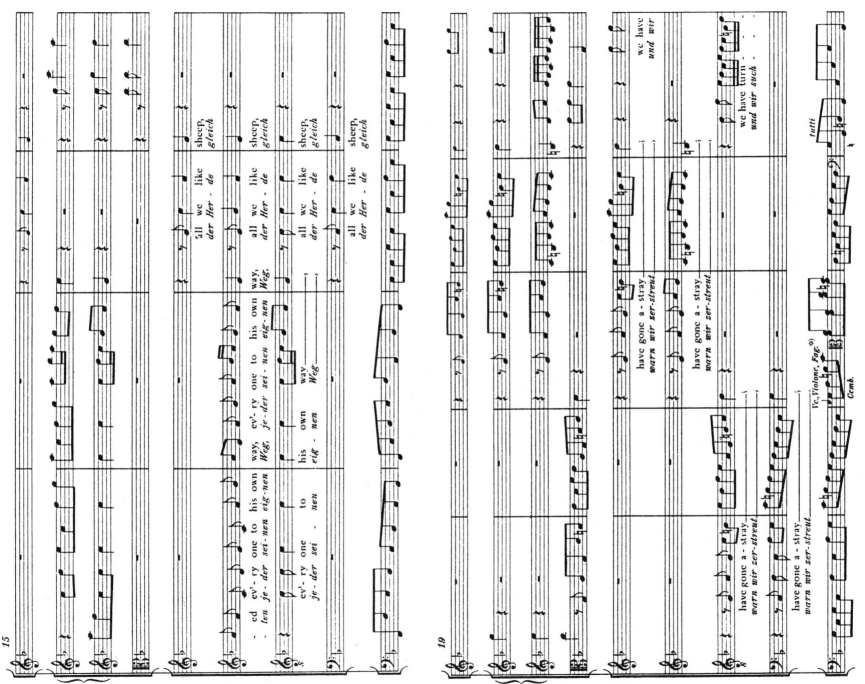

*) Vc., Violone, Fag. pausieren nach dem Viertel g bis zu dem *tutti* in T. 23.

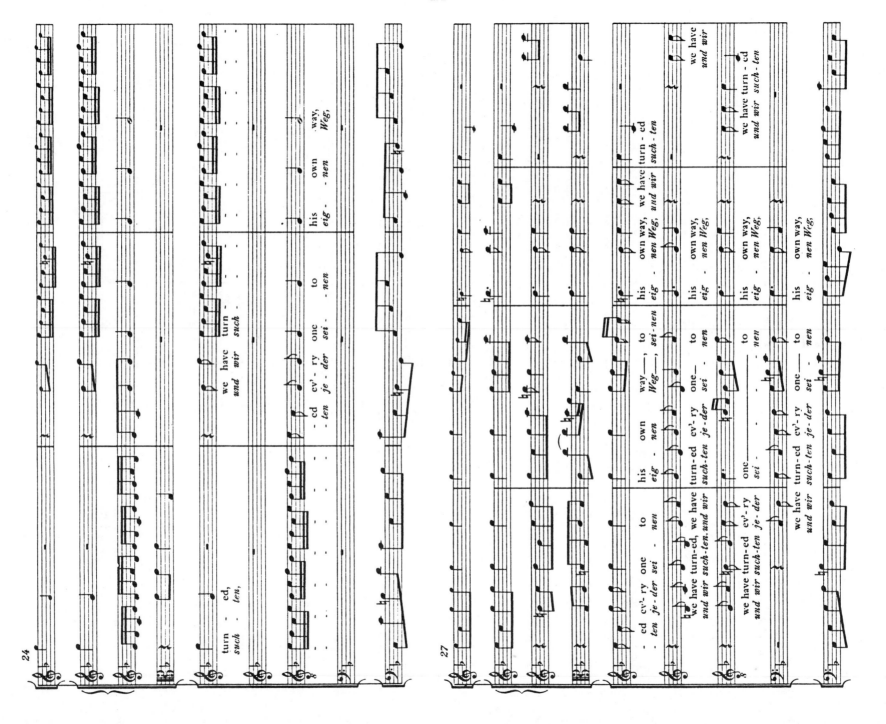

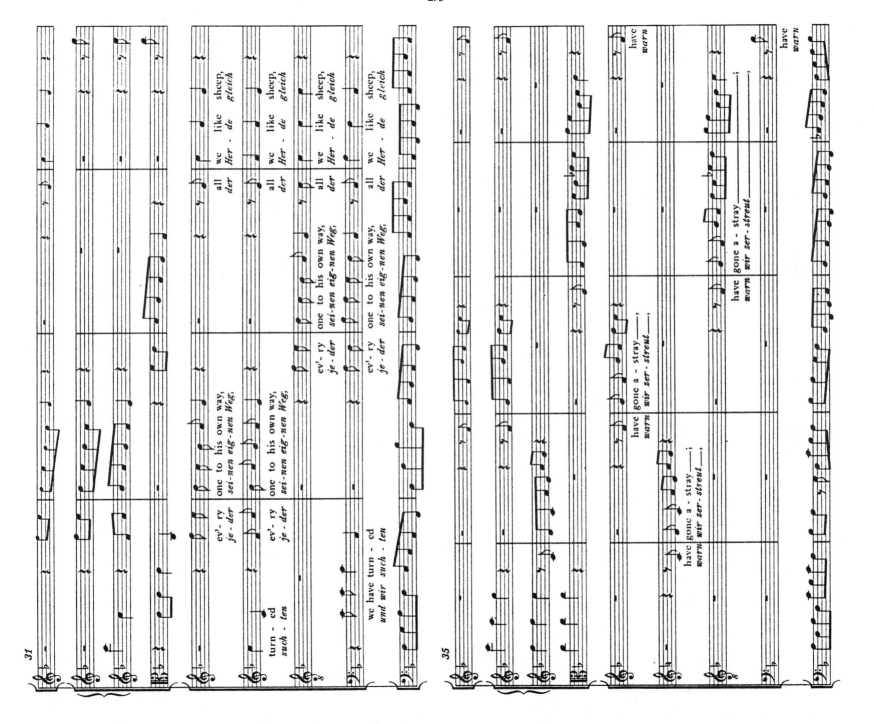

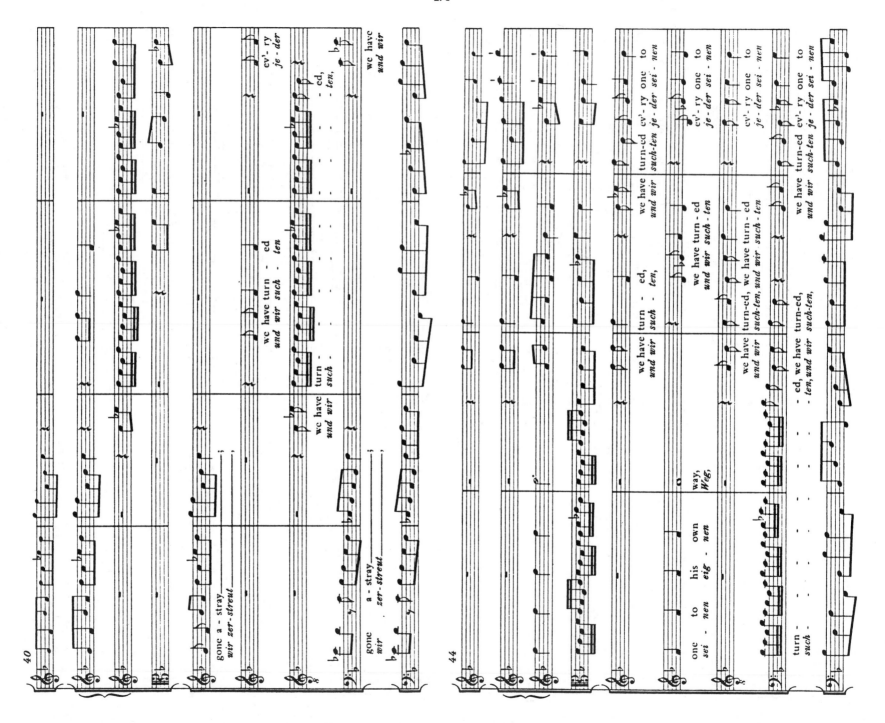

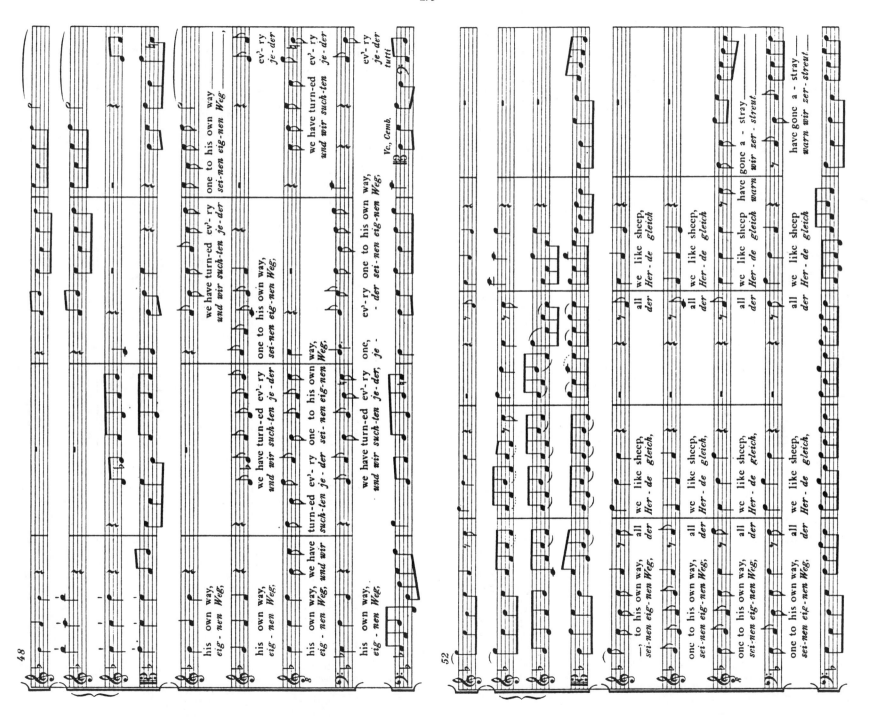

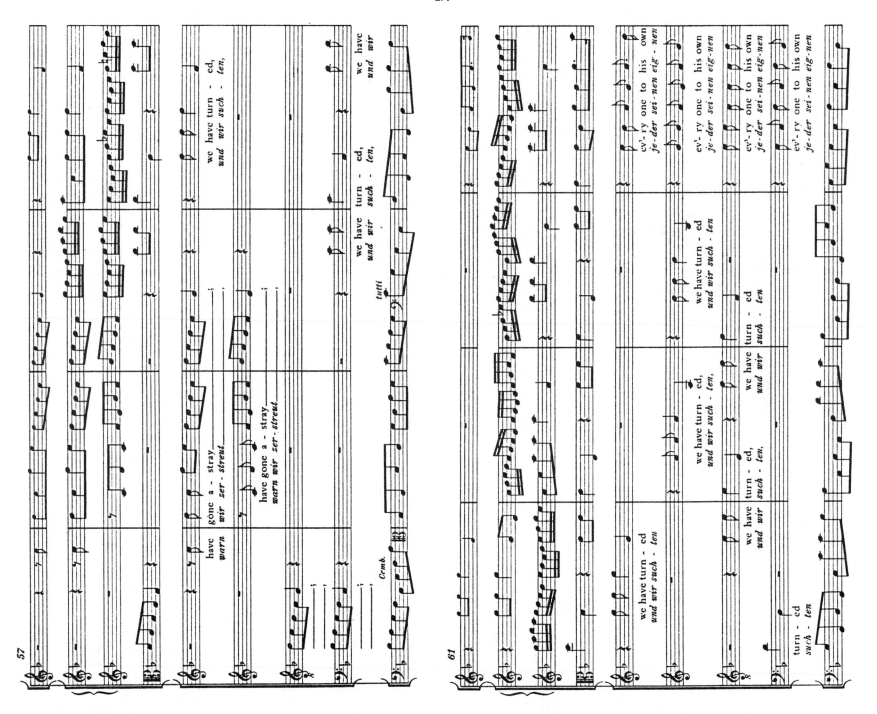

276

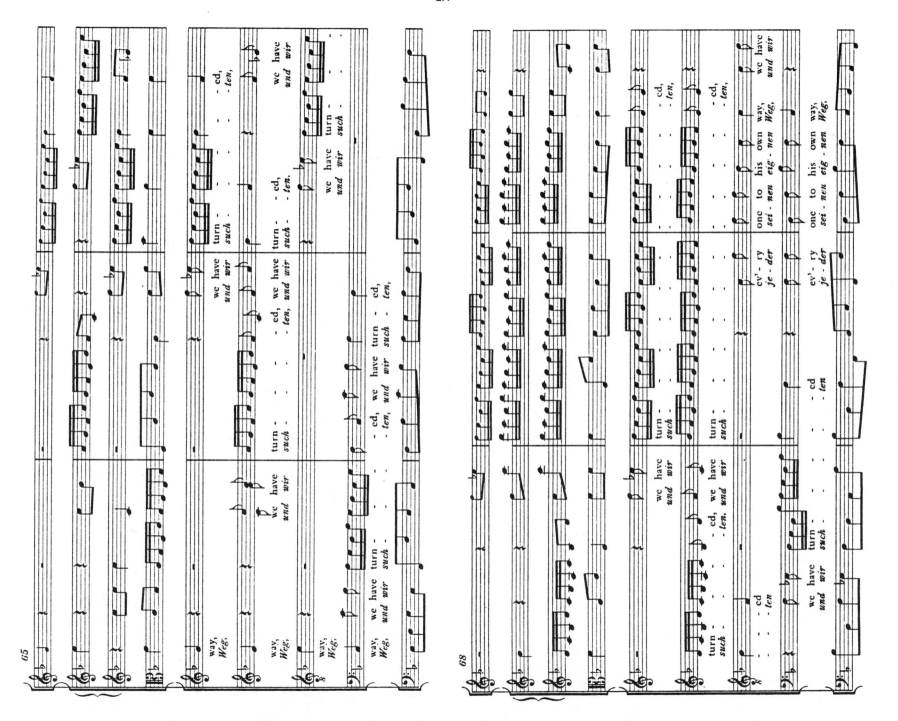

278

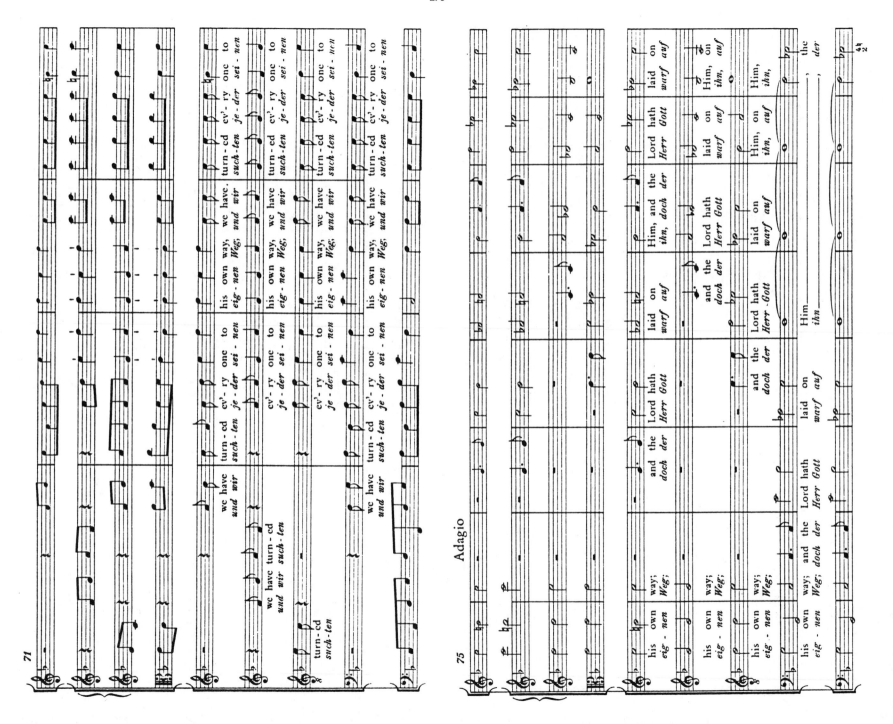

83
Him, hath laid on Him, on Him the in - i - qui - ty of us all.
ihn, er warf auf ihn, auf ihn uns - re Sün - de und Mis - se - - tat.
Him, hath laid on Him the in - i - qui - ty of us all.
ihn, er warf auf ihn uns - re Sün - de und Mis - se - - tat.
hath laid on Him the in - i - qui - ty of us all.
er warf auf ihn uns - re Sün - de und Mis - - se - tat.
Lord hath laid on Him the in - i - qui - ty of us all.
Herr Gott warf auf ihn uns - re Sün - de und Mis - - se - tat.

116. SONATA IN D MAJOR, K. 119 (Longo 415)
Domenico Scarlatti (1685–1757)

117. SYMPHONY NO. 3, in F Major, H. 665 (W. 183), mvt. 1
C. P. E. Bach (1714-1788)

Source: Breitkopf and Härtel, Wiesbaden, Germany.

*The music proceeds directly into the Larghetto second mvt.

118. SYMPHONY NO. 32, in F Major
Giovanni Battista Sammartini (1701-1775)

I

From the publishers of *The Thematic Catalog of the Works of Giovanni Battista Sammartini,* edited by Newell Jenkins and Bathia Churgin, Cambridge, Massachusetts. Harvard University Press, Copyright © 1968 by the President and Fellows of Harvard College. Reprinted by permission.

*m. 35: In mm. 35-36, the octave skips in the manuscript are reversed, starting with the upper octave and descending.

II

* m. 6:  in vn. II. However, the rhythmic differentiation of the cadence here and in m. 36 seems to be deliberate and should be preserved.

292

'mm. 55, 58: bb tied over in the manuscript.

III

Allegro assai

*mm. 54, 56: b♮ d♯ b in the manuscript. Eighths 2-3 are clearly a step too high. The first eighth could either be *a*, as given, or possibly *bb* (which, however, makes an augmented second with c♯).

119. SINFONIA a 8, No. 1, in D Major, mvt. 1
Johann Václav Anton Stamitz (1717-1757)

N.B. The small notes are variants in the Paris edition.

120. LA SERVA PADRONA, Duetto: "Lo conosco"
Giovanni Battista Pergolesi (1710-1736)

From Edwin F. Kalmus and Company, Inc., Boca Raton, FL. Reprinted by permission.

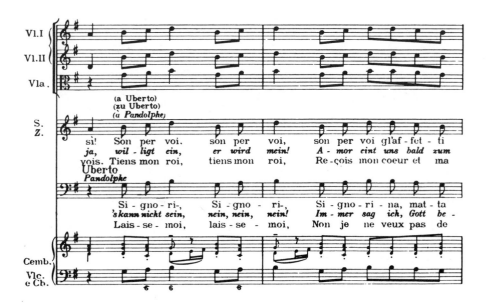

Vl.I
Vl.II
Vla.
S.
Z.
ne-sco, sì, a que - gl'oc chiet-ti, fur - bi, la - dri, ma -
ste-he, ja, wie die - se Blik - ke schel - misch blin-zeln vol -
vi-ne Oui à cet - te mi - ne, à cet - te mi - ne, à cet -
Cemb.
Vlc.
e Cb.
Uberto
Pandolphe
- li-gnet - ti! Si-gno - ri - na, Si-gno-ri - na,
- ler Tük - ke. Schö-ne Don - na, schö-ne Don - na,
- te mi - ne. Ma di - vi - ne, ma di-vi - ne,
Serpina
Zerbine
U.
P.
v'in-gan-na - te! No, no, no, no, che se ben, che se
das sind Träu - me! Nein, nein, nein, nein, sagt der Mund auch zur
Il n'en est rien. J'entends bien j'en-tends bien, Mon mi-gnon mon mi -
ben, che se ben voi di - te no, pur m'ac - cen - na - no di
Stund zehn - mal nein, die Äu - ge - lein la - den doch zur Lie - be
gnon, Vous a - vez beau di - re non, Mais ce n'est pas tout de

SERPINA:

Lo conosco, lo conosco a que gl'
    occhietti, a que gl' occhietti,
furbi, ladri, ladri, malignetti,
che seben voi dite no, no, no,
pur m'accennano di sì, sì, sì,
pur m'accennano di sì!

UBERTO:

Signorina, signorina, v'ingannate,
    v'ingannate!
Troppo, troppo, troppo, in alto voi
    volate!

SERPINA:

I know, I know from those little eyes,
    from those little eyes,
roguish, thieving, robbing, mischievous,
that although you say no, no, no,
you show me signs of yes, yes, yes,
you indicate to me, yes!

UBERTO:

Signorina, little lady, you are wrong, you
    are mistaken!
Too loud, too much, too loud, lower your
    voice!

Gl' occhi e Dio vi dì con no, no, no.
ed un sogno è questo sì, sì, sì,
ed un sogno è questo sì!

SERPINA:
Ma perchè? Ma perchè?
Non sono io bella, graziosa, e spiritosa?
Su mirate leggiadria, leggiadria!
Vè che brio, che brio,
che maestà, che maestà!

UBERTO: (a parte)
Ah, costei mi va tentando,
quanto và che me la fa, che me la fa?

SERPINA: (a parte)
Ei mi par che va calando, va calando.

Risolvete!

UBERTO:
Eh, vanne via!

SERPINA:
Risolvete!

UBERTO:
Eh, matta sei!

SERPINA:
Son per voi gl' affetti miei,
e dovrete sposarme!
⌈Dovrete, dovrete, dovrete, sposarme,
  sposarme!

UBERTO:
Oh, ch' imbroglio, ch' imbroglio,
  ch' imbroglio,
egl' è per me, egl' è per me!

Together

SERPINA:
Lo conosco, sì, a que gl' occhietti,
furbi, ladri, malignetti!

My eyes and God tell you no, no, no,
and this yes, yes, yes, is a dream,
and this yes is a dream!

SERPINA:
But why? But for what reason?
Am I not lovely, graceful, and witty?
You admire prettiness, elegance!
See, what fire, what sprightliness,
what majesty, what majesty!

UBERTO: (aside)
Ah, this woman is trying [tempting] me,
how far is she going to trick me, to play
  a trick on me?

SERPINA: (aside)
It seems to me that he is weakening, is
  softening.
Resolve it!

UBERTO:
Oh, go away!

SERPINA:
Resolve it!

UBERTO:
Oh, you are insane!

SERPINA:
My love is for you,
and you should marry me!
⌈You should, you ought to, you should,
  marry me, marry me!

UBERTO:
Oh, what intrigue, what sharp practice,
  what an entanglement,
this is for me, this is for me!

Together

SERPINA:
I know, yes, from those little eyes,
roguish, thieving, mischievous!

UBERTO:
Signorina, signorina, v'ingannate!

SERPINA:
No, no, no, no, che se ben, che se ben,
che se ben voi dite no,
pur m'accennano di sì.

UBERTO:
V'ingannate!

SERPINA:
Ma perchè? Ma perchè?
Io son bella, graziosa, spiritosa!

UBERTO: (a parte)
Ah, costei mi va tentando!

SERPINA:
Va calando, sì, sì.
Vè che brio, che brio, che maestà, che
  maestà!

UBERTO:
Quanto và, quanto và, quanto và che me
  la fa?
La ralla, la ralla, la ralla, la ralala!
⌈Eh, vanne via! Eh, matta sei!
Signorina, v'ingannate!
Signorina, no, no!
Oh, ch' imbrogl' egl' è per me!

Together

SERPINA:
Via Signore, risolvete!
Son per voi gl' affetti miei, e dovrete sì,
  sì.

UBERTO:
Quanto và, quanto và, quanto và che me
  la fa!

SERPINA:
Io son bella, graziosa, spiritosa!

UBERTO:
La ralla, la ralla!

UBERTO:
Signorina, signorina, you are mistaken!

SERPINA:
No, no, no, no, indeed, indeed,
indeed, you say no,
still you indicate yes to me.

UBERTO:
You are mistaken!

SERPINA:
But why? For what reason?
I am beautiful, graceful, witty!

UBERTO: (aside)
Ah, this woman is indeed trying me!

SERPINA:
He is weakening, yes, yes.
See, what fire, what sprightliness, what
  majesty, what majesty!

UBERTO:
How far is she going, to play a trick on
  me?
La ra la, la ra la, etc.
⌈Ah, go away! Oh, you are insane!
Signorina, you are mistaken!
Signorina, no, no!
Oh, what a muddle this is for me!

Together

SERPINA:
Come, Lord, settle [the question]!
My love is for you, and it must be yes,
  yes.

UBERTO:
How far is she going, to play a trick on
  me?

SERPINA:
I am beautiful, graceful, witty!

UBERTO:
La ra la, la ra la!

SERPINA:
Vè che brio, vè che brio!

SERPINA:
Indeed, what fire, yes, what fire!

UBERTO:
Oh, ch' imbroglio! Oh, ch' imbroglio!

UBERTO:
Oh, what a muddle! Oh, what intrigue!

SERPINA: (a parte)
Va calando, sì, sì!

SERPINA: (aside)
He is weakening, yes, yes!

SERPINA: (à Uberto)
Son per voi, son per voi, son per voi gl'
affetti miei,
e dovrete, sì, sì, sposarme, sposarme!

SERPINA: (to Uberto)
I am yours, I am yours, my love is
yours, and
it must be yes, yes, marry me, marry
me!

UBERTO:
Signori . . . , signori . . . , Signorina,
matta sei!
Signorina, no, no, no, no!
Oh, ch' imbroglio, ch' imbroglio,
(repeated) egl' è per me, egl' è per
me!

UBERTO:
Signori . . . , signori . . . , signorina,
you are insane!
Signorina, no, no, no, no!
Oh, what an intrigue, what a muddle
this is for me, this is for me!

Together

121. LE DEVIN DU VILLAGE, Act I, Scene I
Jean Jacques Rousseau (1712-1778)

The stage setting has at one side the soothsayer's house, at the other side some trees and foundations, and at the back a hamlet.

Colette, crying and wiping her eyes with her apron.

311

COLETTE: AIR.
J'ai perdu tout mon bonheur,
j'ai perdu mon serviteur.
Colin me délaisse,
Colin me délaisse.

J'ai perdu mon serviteur,
j'ai perdu tout mon bonheur.
Colin me délaisse,
Colin me délaisse.

hélas! il a pu changer!
je voudrais n'y plus songer.

COLETTE: AIR.
I have lost all my happiness,
I have lost my servant.
Colin forsakes me,
Colin forsakes me.

I have lost my servant,
I have lost all my happiness.
Colin forsakes me,
Colin forsakes me.

Alas! he could have changed!
I would rather not think about it any
longer.

hélas! hélas!
hélas! hélas!
il a pu changer,
je voudrais n'y plus songer.

hélas! hélas!
j'y songe sans cesse,
j'y songe sans cesse.

J'ai perdu mon serviteur;
j'ai perdu tout mon bonheur.
Colin me délaisse,
Colin me délaisse.

J'ai perdu mon serviteur;
j'ai perdu tout mon bonheur.
Colin me délaisse,
Colin me délaisse.

RECITATIVE.

Il m'aimait autrefois et ce fut mon
   malheur . . . mais quelle est donc
   celle qu'il me préfère? elle est donc
   bien charmante!
Imprudente bergère, ne crains tu point
   les maux que j'éprouve en ce jour?

Colin a pu changer;
tu peux avoir ton tour . . .
que me sert d'y rêver sans cesse?

Rien ne peut guérir mon amour et tout
   augmente ma tristesse.

AIR.

J'ai perdu mon serviteur;
j'ai perdu tout mon bonheur.
Colin me délaisse,
Colin me délaisse.

Alas! alas!
alas! alas!
He could have changed,
I would rather not think about it any
   longer.

Alas! alas!
I think about it incessantly,
I dream about it incessantly.

I have lost my servant;
I have lost all my happiness.
Colin forsakes me,
Colin forsakes me.

I have lost my servant;
I have lost all my happiness.
Colin forsakes me,
Colin forsakes me.

RECITATIVE.

Once he loved me and this was my
   misfortune . . . but who, then, is the
   one whom he prefers to me? Indeed,
   she is quite charming!
Imprudent shepherdess, do you not fear
   at all the hurt that I am experiencing
   today?
Colin could have changed;
you may have your turn . . .
of what use is it for me to dream about
   it incessantly?
Nothing can cure my love and
   everything increases my sadness.

AIR.

I have lost my servant;
I have lost all my happiness.
Colin forsakes me.
Colin forsakes me.

RECITATIVE.

Je veux le haïr; je le dois . . .
peut-être il m'aime encore . . .
pourquoi me fuir sans cesse?
Il me cherchait tant autrefois.
Le devin du canton fait ici sa demeure;
il sait tout; il saura le sort de mon
   amour.
Je le vois et je veux m'éclaircir en ce
   jour.

—J. J. Rousseau

RECITATIVE.

I want to hate him; I must do it . . .
perhaps he still loves me . . .
why do I flee incessantly?
He used to look for me so much.
The soothsayer of the canton lives here;
he knows everything; he will know the
   fate of my love.
I see him, and I want [this] to be
   clarified today.

122. CONCERTO FOR HARPSICHORD OR PIANO AND STRING ORCHESTRA, Op. 7, No. 5, in E♭ Major, mvt. 1
Johann Christian Bach (1735-1782)

Edited by Ákos Fodor

Source: © Boosey & Hawkes, Inc., NY.

123. CONCERTO NO. 27 FOR PIANO AND ORCHESTRA, in B♭ Major, K. 595, mvt. 1
Wolfgang Mozart (1756-1791)

Cadenza   [improvised], ending:

124. ORFEO ED EURIDICE, Excerpt from Act II, Scene 1
Christoph Willibald Gluck (1713-1787)

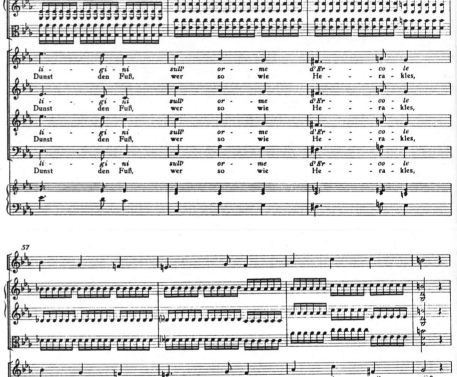

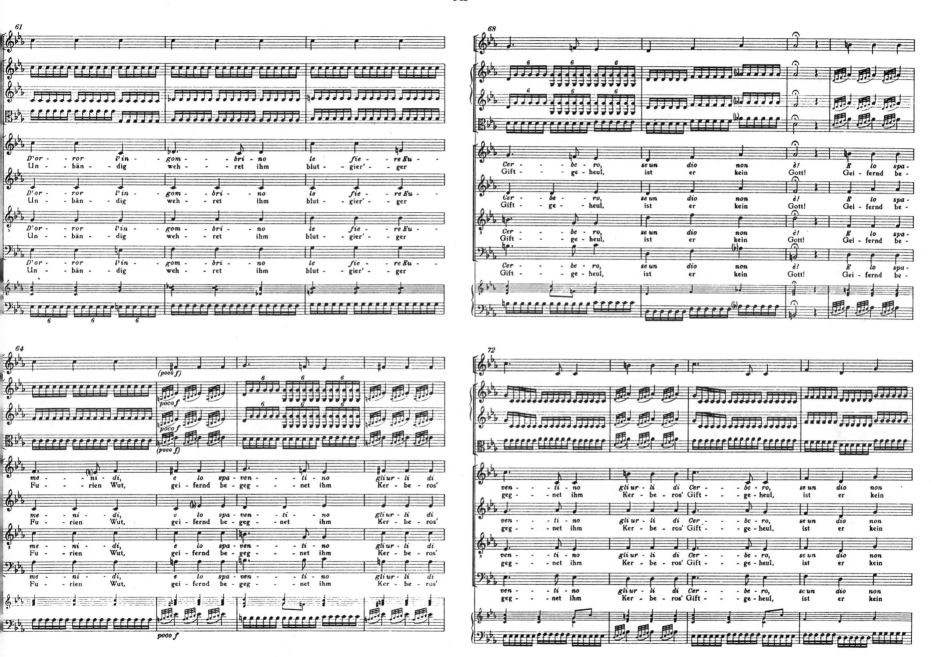

Segue il Ballo, girando intorno ad Orfeo per spaventarlo
Es folgt ein Tanz, Orpheus umkreisend, um ihn zu schrecken

Ballo

[turn quickly]

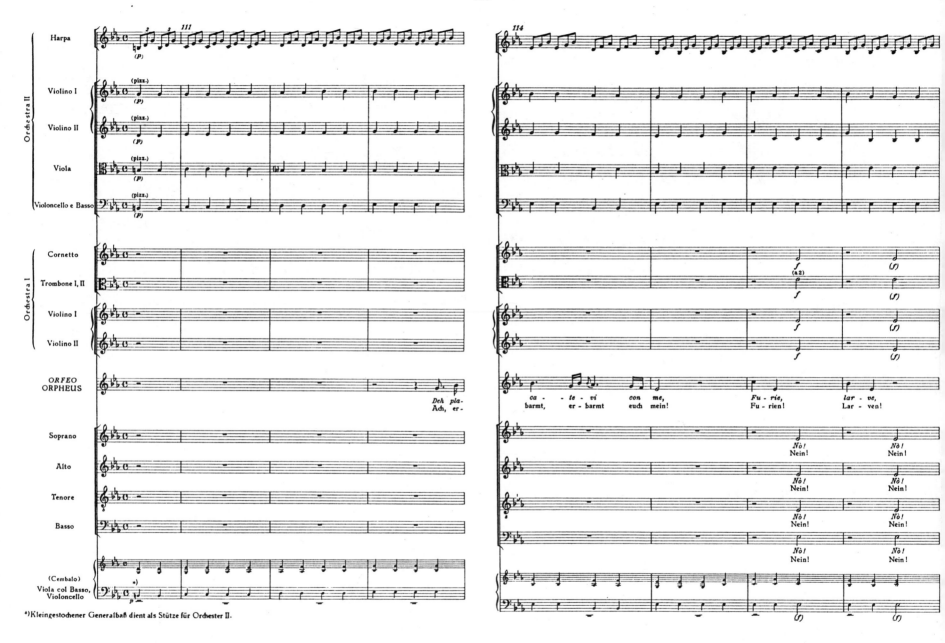

*)Kleingestochener Generalbaß dient als Stütze für Orchester II.

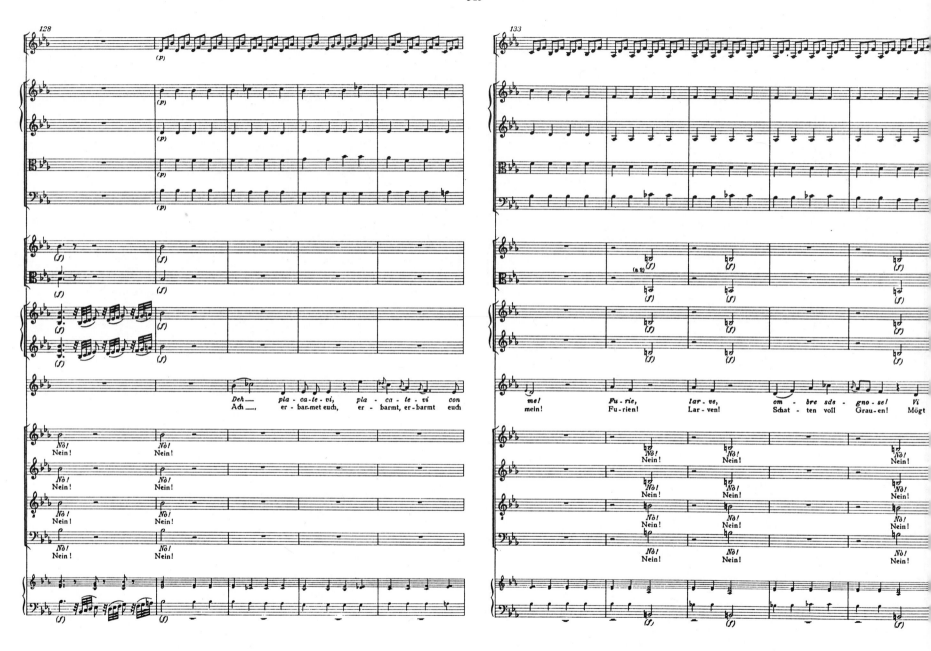

348

CHORUS:

Chi mai dell' Erebo fralle caligini sull' orme d' Ercole e di Piritoo conduce il piè?

D'orror l'ingombrino le fiere Eumenidi, e lo spaventino gli urli di Cerbero, se un dio non è!

E lo spaventino gli urli di Cerbero, se un dio non è!

CHORUS REPEATS STANZA 2; BALLO FOLLOWS

ORFEO:

Deh, placatevi con me.
Furie,   Larve,   Ombre sdegnose!
CHORUS INTERJECTS:
        No!   No!   No!

ORFEO continues:
Vi renda almen pietose
il mio barbaro dolor!
CHORUS: No! No! No!

ORFEO:
Deh, placatevi con me.
Furie,   Larve,   Ombre sdegnose!
CHORUS:
        No!   No!   No!

ORFEO:
Vi renda almen pietose il mio barbaro dolor!
—Raniero de' Calzabigi

CHORUS:

Who would ever set forth from Erebus, through the dark mists, in the footsteps of Hercules and Pirithous?*

He would be obstructed by horror of the bestial Eumenides, ** and he would be frightened by the howling of Cerberus, if he were not a god! And he would be frightened by the howling of Cerberus, if he were not a god!

CHORUS REPEATS STANZA 2; BALLO FOLLOWS

ORFEO:

Oh, please! Be gentle with me.
Furies,   Larvae,   disdainful shadow
CHORUS:
        No!   No!

ORFEO continues:
At least, may my cruel grief
make you merciful!
CHORUS: No! No!

ORFEO:
Oh, please! Be gentle with me.
Furies,   Larvae,   scornful shadows
CHORUS:
        No!   No!

ORFEO:
At least, let my barbarous grief make you merciful!

*Pirithous, King of the Lapithae in Thessaly; friend of Theseus.

**Eumenides, euphemistic term meaning the Gracious Ones, which the Greeks used to refer to the Furies in order to propitiate them.

125. ORFEO ED EURIDICE, Act III, Scene 1, "Che farò senza Euridice?"
Christoph Willibald Gluck (1713-1787)

352

126. SONATA NO. 26, mvt. 2
Franz Joseph Haydn (1732-1809)

Che farò senza Euridice?
Dove andrò senza il mio ben?
Euridice! Euridice!

Oh Dio! Rispondi!
Io son pure il tuo fedel.

Che farò senza Euridice?
Dove andrò senza il mio ben?
Euridice! Euridice!

Ah, non m'avanza più soccorso,
più speranza, nè dal mondo,
nè dal ciel!

Che farò senza Euridice?
Dove andrò senza il mio ben?
—Calzabigi

What will I do without Euridice?
Where will I go without my beloved?
Euridice! Euridice!

Oh, God! Answer!
I am still your faithful one.

What will I do without Euridice?
Where will I go without my beloved?
Euridice! Euridice!

Ah, no more help remains to me,
no more hope, neither from the world,
nor from heaven!

What will I do without Euridice?
Where will I go without my beloved?

Haydn SONATA NO. 26, Movement 2, Lea Pocket Scores. Used by kind permission of European American Music Distributors Corporation, agent for Lea Pocket Scores.

127. STRING QUARTET, Op. 33, No. 2, mvt. 1
Franz Joseph Haydn (1732-1809)

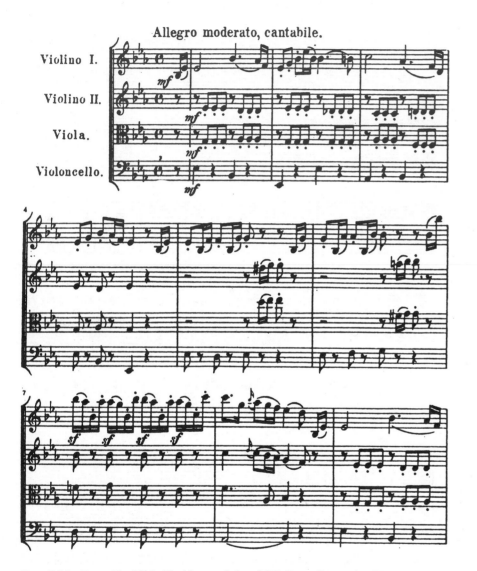

Allegro moderato, cantabile.

Violino I.

Violino II.

Viola.

Violoncello.

128. SYMPHONY NO. 104 (London), in D Major, mvt. 1
Franz Joseph Haydn (1732–1809)

Source: William J. Starr and George F. Devine, *Music Scores, Omnibus*, Part I, *Earliest Music Through the Works of Beethoven.* Copyright © 1964 Prentice-Hall, Inc., Englewood Cliffs, NJ.

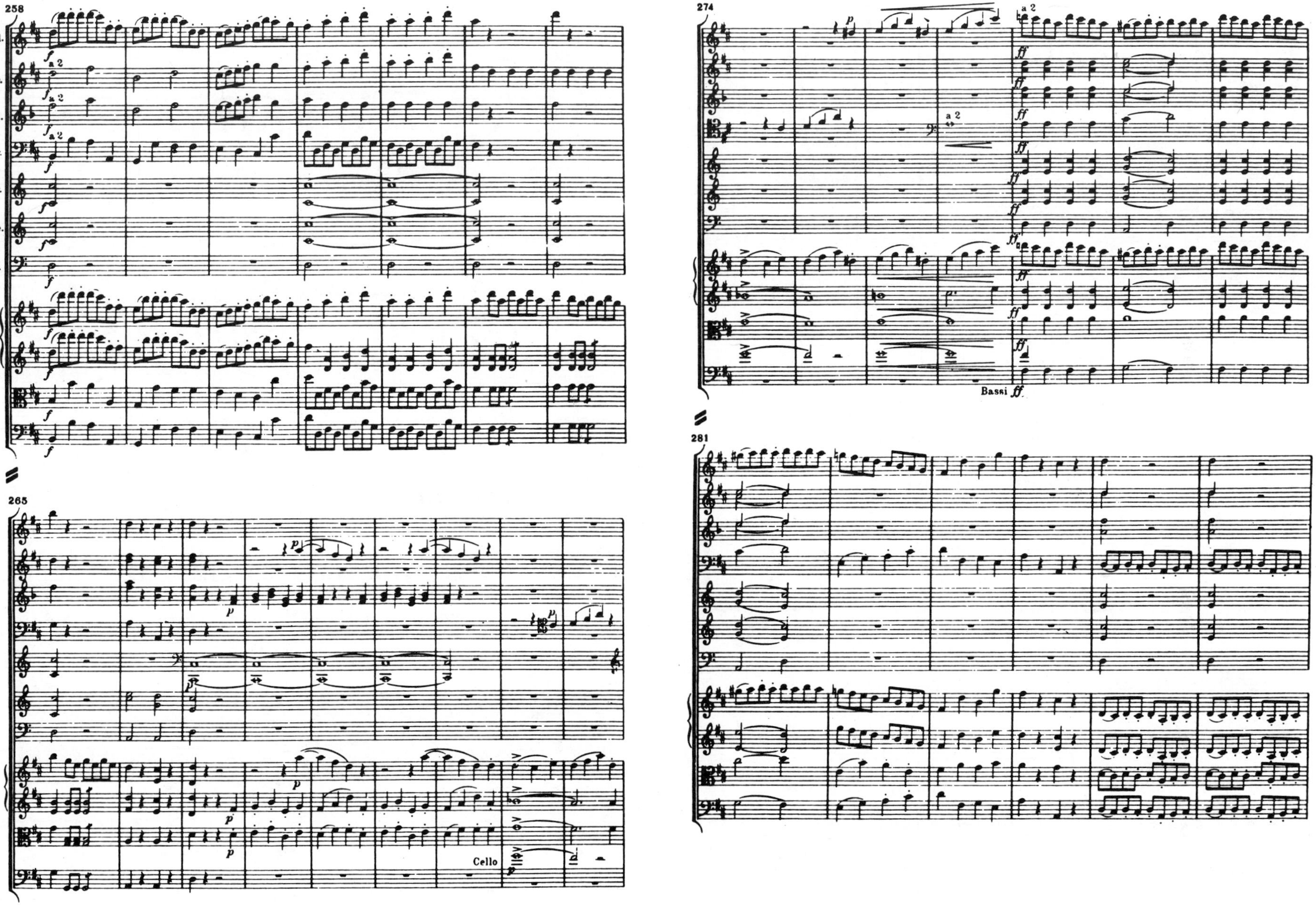
258
Fl.
Ob.
Cl.
Fg.
Cr.
Tbe.
Tp.
a 2
265
Cello
274
a 2
Bassi ff
281

287

129. IL DON GIOVANNI,
Act I, No. 4, Aria: "Madamina"
Wolfgang Mozart (1756–1791)

V'han fra queste contadine, cameriere, citadine,
v'han contesse, baronesse, marchesane, principesse,
e v'han donne d'ogni grado,

d'ogni forma, d'ogni età.

Among these there are peasants, maids, townswomen,
there are countesses, baronesses, marchionesses, princesses,
and there are ladies of every [social] class,
of every figure, of every age.

Nella bionda egli ha l'usanza
di lodarla gentilezza . . .
nella bruna la costanza,
nella bianca la dolcezza.

With blonds he has the habit
of praising gentility . . .
with brunettes, loyalty,
with white-haired ladies, sweetness.

Vuol d'inverno la grassotta,
vuol d'estate la magrotta,
e la grande maestosa,
e la grande maestosa.

In winter he desires the fat one,
in summer he wants the lean one,
and the tall, majestic one,
and the tall, majestic one.

La piccina, la piccina, . . .
    [these 2 words are repeated 6 more times]
è ognor vezzosa;
    [these 3 words are repeated twice more]

The little one, the tiny one, . . .

is always graceful;

Delle vecchie fa conquista
per piacer di porle in lista;

He makes conquest of the old ones
for the pleasure of putting them on the list;

sua passion predominante
è la giovin principante;

his prevailing passion
is the young beginner;

Non si picca, se sia ricca,

It doesn't matter to him, whether she is rich,

se sia bruta, se sia bella,

whether she is ugly, whether she is beautiful,

se sia ricca, bruta,
se sia bella,
purchè porti la gonnella.
Voi sapete quel che fa.
—Da Ponte

whether she is rich, ugly,
whether she is beautiful,
provided she wears the skirt.
You know what he does.

Madamina! Il catalogo è questo,
delle belle, che amò il padron mio!

Little lady! This is the catalog
of the beautiful [women] that my master loved.

Un catalogo egli è ch'ho fatto io:
Osservata, leggete con me!

It is a catalog that I have made:
Observe, read with me!

In Italia sei cento e quaranta,
in Alemagna due cento trent'una;
cento in Francia, in Turchia novant'una,

In Italy, six hundred and forty,
in Germany, two hundred thirty-one;
a hundred in France, in Turkey ninety-one,

ma, ma in Ispagna, son già mille e tre!

but in Spain, there are already a thousand and three!

130. SONATA in C Minor, K. 457
Wolfgang Mozart (1756-1791)

Allegro (after the Autograph)
Molto Allegro (after Artaria and Götz)

* 1st ed.:   . ** 1st ed.:   .

("All the performance indications according to the oldest edition; the Autograph contains them mostly only in the variations of the theme." – B. & H. "Urtext" ed.)

* 1st ed. :

* 1st ed.:

* Artaria and Götz: 𝄽.

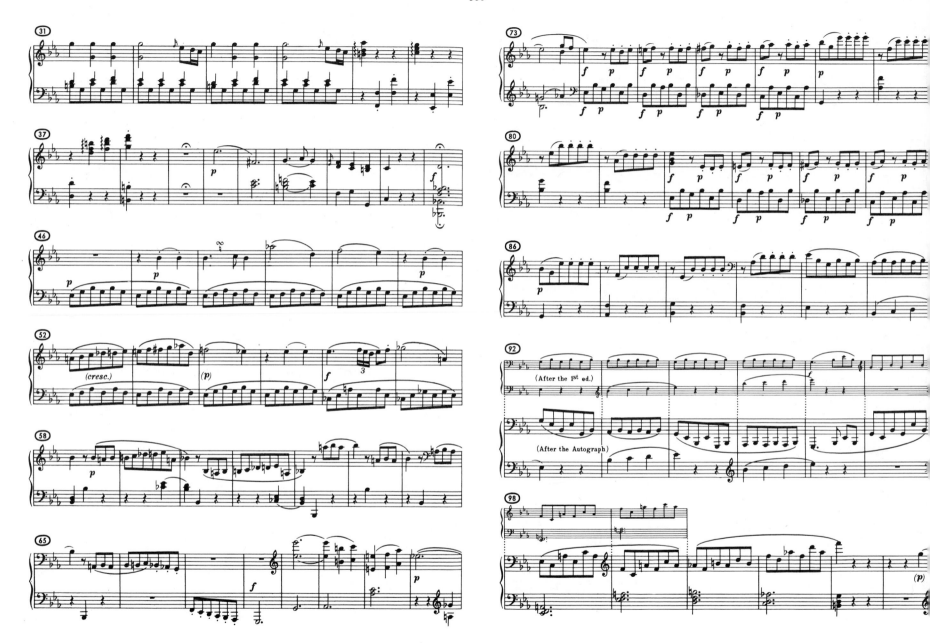

* Artaria and Götz:

131. WHEN JESUS WEPT, Canon
William Billings (1746-1800)

The American Musicology Society and the Colonial Society of Massachusetts.

132. "MY GEN'ROUS HEART DISDAINS," Rondo
Francis Hopkinson (1737-1791)

Reprinted by permission of Da Capo Press, New York, NY.

My gen-'rous heart dis-dains the slave of love to be, I scorn his ser-vile chains, and boast my lib - er - ty. I scorn his ser - vile chains and boast my lib - er - ty. This whining and pin-ing and wasting with care Are not to my taste be she ev - er so fair. This whining and pin-ing and wast-ing with care Are not to my taste be she ev - er so fair.

Shall a girls ca - pri - cious frown Sink my no - ble spir - its down, Shall a face of white and red Make me droop my sil - ly head, Shall I set me down and sigh For an eye - brow

385

133. TRIO IN E♭ MAJOR, Op. 3, No. 1, mvt. 1
for two violins and violoncello
John Antes (1740–1811)

ed. and arr. by Thor Johnson,
Donald M. McCorkle

From *Three Trios*, Copyright © 1961 by Boosey & Hawkes, Inc. Copyright © renewed 1989.

134. ARIA AND ANTHEM
John Antes (1740-1811)

a. "Go, Congregation, Go"

Christian Gregor
(1723-1801)

Edited and arranged by
Donald M. McCorkle

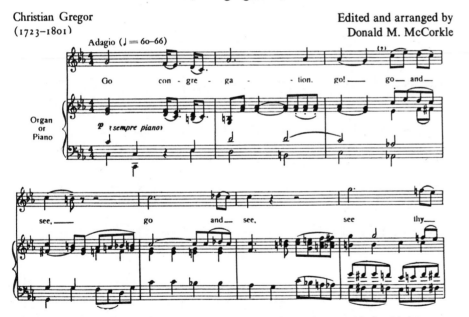

Note: *tr* indicates the points at which double trills (in the top voices simultaneously) are used in the original accompaniment. Since it is impossible to transcribe this device for keyboard, it may be more satisfactory to omit all such trills.

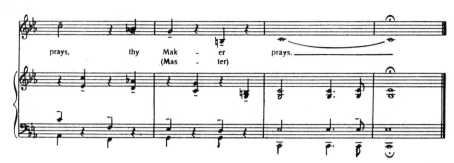

b. "Surely He Has Borne Our Griefs"

Isaiah 53: 4, 5

Edited and arranged by
Donald M. McCorkle

Appendix A: Names of Instruments and Abbreviations

This table sets forth the English, Italian, German, and French names used in music scores for the various musical instruments, together with their respective abbreviations. Presentation is in the arrangement that has become standard in instrumental scores, reading from the top of the score down: Woodwinds, Brass, Percussion, Strings. Those instruments that are used only occasionally are presented last in this table.

Woodwinds

English	Italian	German	French
Piccolo (Picc.)	Flauto piccolo (Fl. Picc.)	Kleine Flöte (Kl. Fl.)	Petite flûte; Flûte piccolo (Fl. picc.)
Flute (Fl.)	Flauto (Fl.); Flauto grande (Fl. gr.)	Grosse Flöte (Fl. gr.)	Flûte (Fl.)
Alto Flute	Flauto contralto (Fl. c-alto)	Altflöte	Flûte en sol
	[pl., Flauti]	[pl., Flöten]	[pl., Flûtes]
Oboe (Ob.)	Oboe (Ob.)	Hoboe (Hb.); Oboe (Ob.)	Hautbois (Hb.)
	[pl., Oboi]	[pl., Hoboen, Oboen]	[pl., Hautbois]
English Horn (E. H.)	Corno inglese (C.; C.i.; Cor. ingl.)	Englisches Horn (Englh.; E. H.)	Cor anglais (C. A.)
Sopranino Clarinet	Clarinetto piccolo (Cl. picc.; Clar. picc.)		
Clarinet (C.; Cl.; Clt.; Clar.)	Clarinetto (Cl.; Clar.)	Klarinette (Kl.)	Clarinette (Cl.)
	[pl., Clarinetti]	[pl., Klarinetten]	[pl., Clarinettes]
Bass Clarinet (B. Cl.)	Clarinetto basso (Cl. b.; Cl. basso; Clar. basso)	Bassklarinette (Bkl.; Bs. Kl.; B.-Kl.)	Clarinette basse (Cl. bs.)
Bassoon (Bsn.; Bssn.)	Fagotto (Fag.; Fg.)	Fagott (Fag.; Fg.)	Basson (Bssn.)
Contrabassoon (C. Bsn.)	Contrafagotto (Cfg.; C. Fag.; Cont. F.)	Kontrafagott (Kfg.)	Contrebasson (C. bssn.; Cbn.)
	[pl., Fagotti]	[pl., Fagotte]	[pl., Bassons]

Brass

English	Italian	German	French
French Horn, or Horn (Hr.; Hn.)	Corno (Cor.; C.)	Horn (Hr.)	Cor; Cor à piston
	[pl., Corni]	[pl., Hörner (Hrn.)]	[pl., Cors]
Trumpet (Tpt.; Trpt.; Trp.; Tr.)	Tromba (Tr.)	Trompete (Tr.; Trp.)	Trompette (Tr.)
	[pl., Trombe]	[pl., Trompeten]	[pl., Trompettes]
Trombone (Tr.; Tbe.; Trb.; Trbe.; Trm.)	Trombone (Tbn.)	Posaune (Ps.; Pos.)	Trombone (Trb.)
	[pl., Tromboni (Tbni.; Trni.)]	[pl., Posaunen]	[pl., Trombones]
Tuba (Tb.)	Tuba (Tb.; Tba.)	Tuba (Tb.); Basstuba (Btb.)	Tuba (Tb.)

Percussion

English	Italian	German	French
Percussion (Perc.)	Percussione	Schlagzeug (Schlag.)	Batterie (Batt.)
Timpani (Timp.); Kettledrums (K. D.)	Timpani (Timp.; Tp.)	Pauken (Pk.)	Timbales (Timb.)
Snare Drum (S. D.)	Tamburo piccolo (Tamb. picc.); Tamburo militaire	Kleine Trommel (Kl. Tr.)	Caisse Claire (C. cl.); Tambour (Militaire) (Tamb. milit.)
Tenor Drum (T. Dr.)	Cassa Rullante	Wirbeltrommel	Caisse Roulante
Bass Drum (B. Dr.)	Gran Cassa (G. C.; Gr. C.; Gr. Cassa)	Grosse Trommel (Gr. Tr.)	Grosse Caisse (Gr. c.)
Cymbals (Cym.; Cymb.)	Piatti (P.; Ptti.; Piat.)	Becken (Beck.)	Cymbales (Cym.)
Tambourine (Tamb.)	Tamburino (Tamb.)	Schellentrommel; Tambourin (Tamb.)	Tambour de Basque (T. de B.; Tamb. de B.; Tamb. de Basque)
Triangle (Trgl.)	Triangolo (Trgl.)	Triangel	Triangle (Triang.)
Tam-tam; Gong (Tam-T.)	Tam-tam	Tam-tam	Tam-tam
Orchestra Bells; Glockenspiel (Glsp.)	Campanelli (Cmp.)	Glockenspiel (Glsp.)	Jeu de Timbres; Carillon
Tubular Bells; Chimes	Campane (Cmp.)	Glocken	Jeu de Cloches; Cloches
Antique Cymbals; Crotales (Crot.)	Piatti antichi; Crotali	Zimbeln; Antiken Zimbeln	Cymbales Antiques; Crotales
Xylophone (Xyl.)	Xilofono	Xylophon	Xylophone (Xyl.)
Siren			Sirène
Cowbells	Cencerro	Kuhlglocken; Herdenglocken	Sonnailles
Wood Blocks (W. Bl.)	Blocco de Legno Cinese	Holzblock	Bloc de Bois
Castanets	Castagnette	Kastagnetten	Castagnettes

Strings

English	Italian	German	French
Violin (V.; Vln.; Vi.)	Violino (V.; Vl.; Vln.)	Violine (V.; Vl.; Vln.) Geige (Gg.)	Violon (V.; Vl.; Vln.)
Viola (Va.; Vl.) [pl., Vas.]	Viola (Va.; Vla.) [pl., Viole (Vle.)]	Bratsche (Br.)	Alto (A.)
Violoncello; 'Cello (Vcl.; Vc.)	Violoncello (Vc.; Vlc.; Vcllo.)	Violoncell (Vc.; Vlc.)	Violoncelle (Vc.)
Double Bass (D. Bs.)	Contrabasso (Cb.; C.B.) [pl., Contrabassi; Bassi (C. Bassi; Bi.)]	Kontrabass (Kb.)	Contrebasse (C.-B.)

Other Instruments Used Occasionally

When included in the orchestra, notation for these instruments is usually placed in the score between percussion and strings.

English	Italian	German	French
Harp (Hp.; Hrp.)	Arpa (A.; Arp.)	Harfe (Hrf.)	Harpe (Hp.)
Piano (Pno.)	Pianoforte (P-f.; Pft.)	Klavier (Kl.)	Piano
Celeste (Cel.)	Celesta	Celesta	Célesta
Harpsichord	Cembalo	Cembalo	Clavecin
Organ (Org.)	Organo	Orgel	Orgue

Appendix B: Some Technical Terms Frequently Used in Orchestral Scores

English	Italian	German	French
Muted; With mute(s)	Con sordino	mit Dämpfer; Gedämpft (for horns)	Sourdine(s)
Take off mutes	Via sordini	Dämpfer(n) Weg	Enlevez les sourdines
Without mute	Senza sordino	Ohne Dämpfer	Sans sourdine
Divided	Divisi (div.)	Geteilt (get.)	Divisé(e)s (div.)
Divided in 3 parts (or whatever number is specified)	div. a 3	Dreifach	div. à 3
In unison (unis.)	Unisono (unis.)	Zusammen	Unis
Solo	Solo	Allein	Seul
All	Tutti	Alle	Tous
(First player only) 1.	1°	1ste; einfach	1er
1., 2. (first and second players on separate parts)	1°, 2°	1ste, 2te	1er, 2e
a2 (2 players on same part)	a2	zu 2	à 2
Near the bridge	Sul ponticello	am Steg	Sur le chevalet
Bow over the fingerboard	Sul tastiera; Sul tasto	am Griffbrett	sur la touche
With the wood of the bow	Col legno	mit Holz; col Legno	Avec le bois
At the point of the bow	Punta d'arco	Spitze	Pointe; de la pointe
At the frog of the bow	al Tallone	am Frosch	du talon
Half (half of a string section is to play)	la metà	die Hälfte	la moitié
Stopped (horns)	Chiuso; chiusi	Gestopft	Bouché; bouchés
Open	Aperto; aperti	Offen	Ouvert
With soft stick; with soft mallet	Bacchetta di spugna	mit Schwammschlegel	Baguette d'éponge; baguette molle
With hard stick(s)	Bacchette di legno	mit Holzschlegeln	Baguette(s) en bois
(Directive to change tuning, or instrument):			
Change C to E	Sol Muta in Mi	C nach E umstimmen	Changez Do en Mi
Change to piccolo (or whatever instr.)	Muta in Piccolo	Piccolo nehmen	Changez en piccolo
Stand, or Desk	Leggio	Pult	Pupitre
Ordinary; In ordinary way (play in ordinary manner, after having played sul ponticello, for example)	Modo ordinario	Gewöhnlich	Mode ordinaire; position nat.

Index